A HISTORY OF PROSTITUTION
FROM ANTIQUITY
TO THE PRESENT DAY

AMS PRESS
NEW YORK

"It was against my principles, but I find that principles have no real force except when one is well fed."

—*Mark Twain.*

A HISTORY OF PROSTITUTION

FROM ANTIQUITY TO THE PRESENT DAY

BY

GEORGE RYLEY SCOTT

F.R.A.I., F.Ph.S. (Eng.), F.Z.S.

LONDON

T. WERNER LAURIE LTD
COBHAM HOUSE
24-26 WATER LANE, E.C.4

Library of Congress Cataloging in Publication Data

Scott, George Ryley, 1886-
    A history of prostitution from antiquity to the
present day.

    Rev. ed. published in 1968 under title: Ladies
of vice.
    Reprint of the 1936 ed. published by T.W. Laurie,
London.
    Includes index.
    1. Prostitution—History. I. Title.
HQ111.S35   1976   301.41'54'09   72-11291
ISBN 0-404-57496-3

From the edition of 1936, London
First AMS edition published in 1976
Manufactured in the United States of America

AMS PRESS, INC.
NEW YORK, N.Y.

CONTENTS

1955220

PREFACE

SOME years ago, in connection with another work, I had occasion to dig deeply into the literature connected with prostitution. I was amazed to find that there was in existence no modern comprehensive study of a sociological phenomenon which is of the most profound significance. The only two works which can be called in any sense of the word exhaustive are those of Sanger and Lacroix. Both are hopelessly out of date. Sanger died in 1872 ; Lacroix's two-volume work was published in 1851. To-day these obese tomes are of little more than historical value.

There are other more modern works, but for the most part they are fragmentary, prejudiced studies dealing with special phases of prostitution, or with its relation to other sociological factors. In many cases they are issued by, or with the aid of, societies for promoting some reform or other, or with the object of alleviating an evil, and in consequence they are frankly propagandistic in tone and treatment. Their approach to the subject of prostitution is not a direct approach—it is rather a consideration of the social evil as something which the writer is forced to include in an examination or a study devoted to some far worthier matter. This attitude colours the whole study and largely nullifies its force and value.

The reason for this is not far to seek. Prostitution is one of those subjects the discussion of which has always been either evaded altogether, or justified and excused by being linked up with some praiseworthy social object or reform. Acton, an Englishman, writing in 1857, prefaced his work with a meandering sanctimonious apology ; Sanger, an American, wrote an introduction to his *History of Prostitution* which was a masterpiece of piaculous sophistry ; Lacroix, a Frenchman, when he had completed his work, jibbed at letting his own name appear on the title page, and published the book under the pseudonym of Pierre Dufour. Even in these sophisticated days, when writers have surprisingly few scruples, most authors are averse to tackling a subject which is still generally looked upon as unsavoury.

Now, whenever I take up a book and find it prefaced with an excuse or an apology, I am, rightly or wrongly, immediately prejudiced against both the book and its writer. I cannot disabuse my mind of the impression that an author who has to adopt such tactics will be afraid to deal with his subject adequately, or to tackle it fearlessly.

In submitting this study of prostitution I make no excuse for it ; I offer no apology. I am not connected, officially or otherwise, with any reformative, moralistic, or pietistic society or association. I believe the need exists for a work surveying the whole field of prostitution, not with the jaundiced eye of the reformer or moralist, but with the dispassionate eye of the scientific observer.

GEORGE RYLEY SCOTT.

PART I

THE CAUSES OF PROSTITUTION

A HISTORY OF PROSTITUTION

CHAPTER I

THE QUESTION OF DEFINITION

It is a capital error to start an examination without defining exactly what one intends to examine. It is essential, before we can deal with prostitution, that we should know exactly what a prostitute is.

Writers on the subject in the past have differed widely in their attempts at definition. Paul Lacroix classed as prostitutes all women who were guilty of intercourse outside the married state ; similarly Wardlaw, writing in 1842, defined prostitution as "the illicit intercourse of the sexes." On the other hand the popular conception of a prostitute as a woman who temporarily loans the use of her body to a miscellany of men in return for money is obviously too narrow and restricted ; as is also Webster's dictionary definition, "to give up to lewdness for hire." In most cases essential factors to come within the meaning of prostitution are held to be immoral relations with at least two men contemporaneously, and for gain in each case.

It is as important to differentiate between a mistress and a prostitute as it is to differentiate

3

between a married woman and a prostitute. The woman who lives with a man for an extended period, even though she forsakes him or is forsaken by him, and becomes the mistress of another man, is no more a prostitute, at this particular stage in her life, than a married woman who obtains a divorce and marries another man is a prostitute. She may have been a prostitute before or she may become one later, but this does not affect the point. Thus to include mistresses in the category of prostitutes, is to give to prostitution too wide a scope. Actually these points may not be of any great practical importance in England ; but in France and in certain other countries where prostitutes are inscribed, the distinction is one of considerable significance.

On the other hand, to limit prostitution to those who are entirely dependent for their livelihood upon promiscuous intercourse is at once too narrow and too illogical a definition. For these constitute but a fractional part of the vast army of women who indulge in promiscuous sexual relations as a side-line or a part-time occupation, and in many instances for other reasons than those connected with pecuniary reward. The distinction between the amateur and the professional is always conceded to be a distinction of money. In its ultimate analysis it is a meaningless distinction. It overlooks the fact that one may be willing to do something, whether distasteful or not does not matter, for some form of reward or recompense other than coin of the realm. Money is merely a token. The wealthy hobbyist or amateur has invariably some " object " other than pure altruism. The fact that there is no cash transaction does not necessarily mean the work, in popular parlance, is done for nothing.

These amateur prostitutes, as they may be conveniently called, are increasing in all civilised countries, year by year, and, as we shall see, are continually intruding more and more upon the professional prostitutes' preserves.

The contention that the disgust associated with prostitution in the mind of any respectable member of society really lies in the sex-lust which manifests itself in every transaction, and not in the mere fact that it is a trade, fails to take into account that the same argument applies to many State- and Church-authorized marriages ; just as the other contention that there can be no act of prostitution where a monetary transaction does not take place overlooks the fact that few marriages are free from financial taint and economic considerations.

Any true definition, in contradistinction to a legal definition, of a prostitute, would embrace both the professional and the amateur fornicator. The law and, in the main, the Church and the public, in their rulings, take no cognisance of anyone other than the woman who makes a living exclusively out of promiscuity. The popular supposition that the role of marriage precludes the possibility of prostitution, while in accordance with the law's interpretation, seems at variance with an ethical or a sociological viewpoint.

In indulging in promiscuous intercourse the prostitute is influenced in part or whole by some incentive other than or in addition to love or passion. The prostitute is seldom a nymphomaniac, though the nymphomaniac may become a prostitute. Nor does the absence of love from the prostitute's professional dealings imply that she is incapable of love. The twin popular assumptions that every prostitute is a volcano of lust towards all the men she can attract, and coincidentally incapable of feeling anything resembling love for any individual man, are both fallacies. It is because the prostitute, despite the fact that she may be loaning her body to man after man without any voluptuous sensations, is capable of feeling real love for one individual man that, in some cases, is explainable the apparently inexplicable fact that it is common enough for a prostitute to herself keep what is termed a " fancy man."

Many observers contend that the absence of the love element is the one essential factor that stamps the woman as a prostitute. It is argued that a vital element in prostitution is that the woman derives no pleasure from her sexual escapades, but is concerned solely with the fees she receives in return for her services.

It seems to me, however, that the question of pleasure or otherwise cannot logically or justifiably enter into any definition of what constitutes a prostitute. Further there appears to be little in the way of actual facts to support this assumption of universal insensibility, and even the microscopic amount which does exist seems to be founded upon the most dubious premises. We all know well enough that every pleasure loses its pristine flavour if it is repeated often enough or continued long enough, and there is not the smallest doubt that prostitutes who have followed the profession for years on end can derive little or no pleasure from the sexual relations to which they are so accustomed. But then it is doubtful if many married women, after regular repetitive sexual relations over a long period of years, get any pleasure from the act. The crux of the matter lies in the question of whether the prostitute, *at the commencement of her career, derives pleasure from the sex act?* And the answer, I venture to submit, is that in nine instances out of ten she does experience pleasure. She makes, in many cases, a point of combining business with pleasure, to the extent of selecting for her partners in sexual enjoyment those willing to bestow upon her money or its equivalent.

Pleasure in connection with the sex act does not necessarily imply love. Love is entirely another thing. Most men who resort to prostitutes for sexual satisfaction experience pleasure, but relatively few fall in love with the women who are mainly instrumental in providing this pleasure. The prostitute, once she is regularly embarked upon her career, rarely experiences love in the course of her work.

The female harlot, therefore, in contradistinction to the married woman (in theory, at any rate) and to the mistress, offers the use of her body to various men in exchange for money or its equivalent, and apart from or in addition to any thought of love. In many instances she goes through the sexual act and its concomitants devoid of any pleasurable feelings whatever ; often, indeed, her feelings for her temporary lover are dislike or even hatred. That she performs her part in the transaction competently and apparently passionately is not, as is so often thought, evidence of her sensuality or lust ; it is merely a tribute to her skill as a professional love-maker.

It is true that many married women have no feelings of love for their husbands even at the time of marriage ; it is equally true that soon after marriage thousands of wives develop frigidity and *anaesthesia sexualis* towards the men they are supposed to love. In these cases the only thing that distinguishes the role of such a woman from that of a prostitute is that *one* man has contracted for the use of her body, and that the contract is sanctioned and upheld by Church and State.

There is, too, the question of the male prostitute. Prostitution is not exclusively a woman's profession ; nor are those who consort with and support prostitutes exclusively members of the male sex. Male prostitutes, often euphemistically described as gigolos, are employed and paid by women ; catamites are employed by homosexual and perverted men. Thus our definition of a prostitute must include both sexes, and bearing this essential point in mind as well as our previous observations, we arrive at the following : A prostitute is an individual, male or female, who for some kind of reward, monetary or otherwise, or for some form of personal satisfaction, and as a part- or whole-time profession, engages in normal or abnormal sexual intercourse with various persons, who may be of the same sex as, or the opposite sex to, the prostitute.

CHAPTER II

THE SOCIAL STANDING OF THE PROSTITUTE

To-day men and women of respectability alike look upon the prostitute with contempt or pity, or both. Even men who are largely responsible for the profession's existence, and who affect the society of its practitioners in drinking lounges and night clubs, when in the company of female relatives or friends, refrain from any discussion of prostitution, are studiously careful not to patronise any cafés which cater for women of easy virtue, and greet with icy stares the *filles de joie* with whom they have spent the previous night. The prostitute is often referred to as a " moral outcast," and, generally speaking, the reaction of polite society to her is analogous to its reaction towards an ugly family skeleton which one would like to bury decently.

So universal is this attitude that it is not unnatural there is an impression abroad that this same reaction towards the prostitute has always been current. It is a mistaken assumption. The prostitute's profession has not always been a shameful profession. To the contrary, at one time the harlot was an object of reverence and adoration, as

9

anyone who is well acquainted with the Bible and contemporary literature should know. In fact, at one time, in certain races, according to Lord Avebury, prostitutes were in even higher regard than were legitimately married women. →In Athens they held the highest possible rank ; in Vesali, too, the " chief of the courtesans " received a degree of veneration approaching that given to those of holy or chieftain blood. Even to-day, in China and Japan, and among certain primitive races, the profession of the prostitute is not one of shame.

The *Kedeshoth* mentioned in the Bible were prostitutes attached to the Canaanite temples, and were held in the highest reverence by the worshippers. Temple prostitutes, in all countries, and at all times, have been highly thought of, and in cases where this service to their god was of a temporary nature, found no difficulty in effecting marriages. According to Strabo, among the ancient Armenians, who prostituted their daughters to the service of their god, these temporary harlots married without the slightest smudge upon their characters. Again the Babylonian women were similarly not looked down upon. To the contrary they were considered to be women who, in the true spirit of religious devotion, sacrificed their lives to the service of their god ; and as such received a degree of veneration and of respect that is usually reserved for those moving in the most exalted circles.

All of which goes to show that the practice of professional prostitution under the license of religion was viewed through a vastly different pair of spectacles from those which are turned upon it to-day.

But I shall have more to say on this subject when I come to deal with sacred prostitution in a later stage of this inquiry.

In Japan the prostitute is not looked down upon as she is in all European countries. No vulgar or derogatory terminology is used in referring to her. For instance, there is not, in the Japanese language, anything equivalent to the English whore* or harlot. The word which we translate as prostitute really signifies " temporary wife." Many of the girls attached to the *maisons de plaisir* in Japan, in later years marry and live in conditions of the utmost respectability.

In India prostitutes were never looked upon as in any sense of the word degraded or immoral creatures. According to Meyer, " the Hindu has always sung the praises of ' the public woman ' as the very type and embodiment of perfect womanhood."**

Much of this toleration of intercourse outside the married state is due to the males in many primitive races valuing neither virginity itself nor the exclusive right to sexual connection with any particular woman. [In many savage tribes, as a mark of honour, a male guest is allowed by the husband or father to sleep with his wife or his daughter.]

* The word " whore," although widely employed in England, and particularly in early literature, is, according to the writer of the article on " Prostitution " in *The Encyclopaedia Britannica* (eleventh edition), not Anglo-Saxon at all, but comes from Scandinavia, being derived from the earlier forms " hore " and " hoore." When the revised version of the New Testament was prepared, " harlot " was substituted wherever " whore " appeared in the older version.

** Johann Jakob Meyer, *Sexual Life in Ancient India*, Routledge. 1930, Vol. I, p. 264.

With the advent of civilisation and the patriarchal system such a thing became plainly intolerable. But, recognising that, to the majority of men, the provision of a temporary love partner constitutes a source of pleasure, in many civilised countries it became customary to provide guests of honour with high-class prostitutes or courtesans. We see evidence of this in the custom in Germany and other countries in the Middle Ages, of giving visiting members of royal houses free entry into the brothels of the city. In 1434, on his visit to Ulm, King Sigismund was escorted through the gates of the city by prostitutes. In the sixteenth century, any foreign envoys visiting the Swiss town of Zurich were entertained at table not by the town officials and their wives but by the town officials and certain picked harlots from the city brothels. And although anything of this nature would not be tolerated to-day, there have been instances, even in recent years, where, in certain foreign cities, on occasions when meetings and conferences were held, the provision of special facilities, or the extension of existing ones, for enabling visitors to come into contact with prostitutes were apparently "overlooked" by the authorities.

Coincidentally with the English concept of degradation and shame is the firmly established idea that every prostitute is necessarily a girl of the feeblest mentality, in many cases little removed from an actual imbecile. Tarnowsky, the Russian authority on sex, held the view that professional prostitutes, as a result of their heredity coupled with arrested or incomplete development, were mental degenerates. Most students of the subject in the past have formed somewhat similar conclusions to that of Tarnowsky. Among more modern researchers, Talmey in a recent edition of his book *Love*, comes to the conclusion that " defective mentality is responsible for the presence of prostitutes."

I am of opinion, however, that there are the strongest grounds for supposing these views to have been greatly exaggerated. For the most part they have been based upon the researches of social, moral, and religious workers, or upon the statistics furnished by Magdalen hospitals, prisons, rescue homes, and the like. In consequence they are drawn from observations concerned with the lowest class of prostitute only, and they give a quite false impression as regards prostitution as a whole. There have always been a very considerable number of prostitutes of normal mentality and education, as anyone who has come in contact with the better class and the more successful women must admit. Dr. Wolbarst, referring to this very matter, says : " We are told that prostitutes are below normal in intelligence. I have had professional dealings with many, and believe this statement is not true."* To-day, whether the fact be palatable or the contrary, the intelligence and education of the prostitute bear favourable comparison with the intelligence and education of those engaged in most pursuits open to women. The standard of education in the ranks of harlotry has risen in the same way as in any other walk of life.

* A. L. Wolbarst : *Generations of Adam*, Werner Laurie, p. 247.

In every consideration of the professional prostitute one must always bear in mind the attitude of
society towards this type of woman. [The prostitute
is a social outcast, decried, sneered at and denounced
by all respectable members of society, both men and
women. The men who patronise harlots and enable
them to live, whatever attitude they adopt in strict
privacy, sneer at them in public.] Woman's
attitude towards the prostitute is slightly different
from man's. In her case, it is not mere disgust or
contempt ; it is disgust tinctured with hatred for
and jealousy of a successful rival. The married
woman cannot rid herself of the idea that the
prostitute is offering something outside marriage,
which is, or should be, an exclusive part of the
marriage contract. The single woman is bothered
by the idea that the street woman is to some extent
spoiling her chances of getting married. It is this
attitude on the part of the female sex which, in
particular, renders of little value studies of prostitution undertaken by women—they are invariably
prejudiced to an extent which causes them to be
either useless or misleading.

Much of the horror associated with prostitution
is more a matter of terminology than of anything
else. It is the word prostitute, or whore, or harlot
that has more to do with arousing feelings of disgust
than the actual promiscuity connected with the
trade. Even the prostitute herself, in many cases,
bursts into hot rage and fiercely resents the appella-
tion of whore. In all circumstances where promiscuity has been considered to be respectable, it has
not been called prostituion. Thus the harlots

attached to Moabite, Canaanite, and Assyrian temples were not called prostitutes at all, but priestesses; it was the Hebrews who referred to them as whores. The *hetairae* of ancient Greece were never referred to, or looked upon, as common harlots. And similarly, down through the ages, the French and Italian courtesans who presided over salons thronged with the intelligentsia of Europe, the mistresses of kings and aristocrats. So true is all this that to-day the mistresses and the divorcees rank as respectable women.

CHAPTER III

THE UNDERLYING CAUSE

THE fundamental cause of female prostitution does not rest with the woman at all ; it rests with the male animal. It is a biological cause. This is never stated bluntly, but it is admitted by implication.

The reasons which induce women to take up prostitution as a career are confused with the basic cause of prostitution itself, which is something quite different. In its essence prostitution is physical. Its existence is due to the physiological urge which drives the virile male animal to search for his mate and to have intercourse with her. It is, stated in plain language, the self-same urge as that which actuates the dog hanging around the bitch which is in heat.

It is this biological urge which has led, during the two thousand years of the Christian era, a miniature army of religious, moral and social leaders to look upon prostitution as an evil which must be endured ; a cancerous sore which can never be eradicated but can only be checked. Always at the back of their minds was the fear that the eradication of prostitution, supposing it were possible, would bring worse evils in its train. It is this viewpoint which causes governments to view with tolerant eyes the " camp followers " of the soldiers during peace and war, and even on occasion to go so far as to provide brothels for the use of troops stationed in colonial and foreign lands.

All through the ages prostitution has presented a knotty problem ; and nothing in all the world has provided a more pronounced subject for the hypocrisy of the theologians and the self-elected guardians of public morals. The difficulty they have always been faced with, and which they are faced with to-day, is to justify the denunciation of something which they consider it would be inadvisable to suppress ; and, in addition, to justify the punishment and ostracism of one party only to a contract, which is conceded to be evil, between two parties. For prostitution exists not because it is impossible to suppress it in the sense that murder, or robbery, or infanticide, is suppressed ; but because no really thorough or sincere attempt has ever been made at suppression. In some countries it is openly regulated ; in others it is curbed, restricted, and, to some extent, curtailed ; <u>in none is it rigidly suppressed</u>.

This attitude of coincident denunciation of something against which only half-hearted measures of regulation or restriction have been taken, has required a certain amount of justification. The plea for toleration of the evil has always taken, despite modern ornamentation, the fundamental lines laid down by Saint Augustine seventeen hundred years ago. He held that the prostitute was an essential member of society. Sinful she was, depraved she was, sordid she was ; but she was required for the express purpose of keeping lust within bounds and in proper channels. Just as Saint Paul before him had contended that although all sexual intercourse was sinful, yet it were better to marry than to " burn " ; so Saint Augustine contended that despite the immorality of all fornication it were better that man should sin with a prostitute for his partner than that he should rape a respectable woman. In his own words : " What is more base, empty of worth, and full of vileness than harlots and other such pests ? Take away harlots from human society and you will have tainted everything with lust. Let them be with the matrons and you will produce contamination and disgrace. So this class of persons, on account of their morals, of a most shameless life, fills a most vile function under the laws of order." Similarly, according to Athenaeus, Solon sanctioned the purchase of female slaves to be used as prostitutes in order to prevent the raping of respectable women ; and Salvianus stated that the Romans established brothels as a preventive of adultery.

On the whole, however, theologians after Saint Augustine's day, contented themselves with wholesale and comprehensive denunciation of all intercourse outside the married state, and where it became necessary to give any explicit opinion, with a denouncement of prostitution generally. Sexual intercourse itself ceased to be a subject for theological denunciation ; and with the sanctifying of marriage the views of Saint Paul and his contemporaries were judiciously ignored, glossed over, or

converted into a specific injunction against intercourse outside the marital state.   Fornication
became the specal purlieu of prostitution and was
condemned unreservedly.

So matters rested until in the early part of the
eighteenth century Mandeville, in his notorious
satire, *The Fable of the Bees*, re-stated the doctrine of
Saint Augustine, propounding the theory that
society was indebted to the prostitute for the safety
of female morals.   A century later others took up
the tale.   Schopenhauer averred that prostitutes
were " human sacrifices on the altar of monogamy ";
Lecky justified the harlot's existence on the grounds
that she was [" the most efficient guardian of
virtue "];   Balzac, writing of prostitutes in his
Physiology of Marriage, said " they sacrifice themselves for the republic and make of their bodies a
rampart for the protection of respectable families."
And others hymned the same tune.   Man's sexual
needs outside marriage, and his polygamous nature,
both of which were admitted by implication if not
explicitly ;   and woman's coincidental need of
protection against man ;   were the justifications for
prostitution which have continued to hold sway
wherever and whenever the problem has received
consideration.

With all this granted, it seems strange that, at
the same time, the true cause of prostitution, and
the fact that man is mainly responsible for its
existence, have not been realised and admitted.   It
seems strange that, after these admissions, students
of the subject should present as the major cause of
prostitution the economic need of woman.   True,

this is a contributory cause (as I shall attempt to show in the next chapter), but it is not the basic cause. The need for woman to earn a living outside orthodox respectable forms of labour, and of marriage, does not mean, as is so often submitted, that prostitution must exist. The real cause is the sexual appetite of man. This appetite creates the demand for fornication outside the married state ; and the fact that man is willing to pay for the means of satisfying his sexual requirements brings into being the professional prostitute. Were man unable or unwilling to pay the price asked there would be no professional prostitutes, but there would be an enormous increase in the number of cases of rape and seduction. Thus Saint Augustine's original dictum, supplemented by Lecky, Schopenhauer, Balzac, *et al*, is dependent upon man being able to pay for his pleasure. The alternative to rape and seduction, in circumstances where economic conditions precluded the payment of the prostitute by her clients, would be the provision of free professional public women by the State either as slaves or paid fornicators.

Man is essentially polygamous, and the development of civilisation extends this innate polygamy. In any society, therefore, where comparatively a small proportion only can afford polygamy, or a succession of wives (which is really polygamy legalised and camouflaged), or a number of mistresses, the majority of men must have recourse to prostitutes, professional or amateur.

Every step forward in civilisation extends man's biological urge for fornication, where it does not express itself along homosexual or perverted lines. Sexual stimulation develops alongside civilisation. It is a fact that domesticated animals have sexual appetites developed far in advance of animals in the wild state. Every zoologist knows the truth of this. It is a fact that the two primary things with which mankind is concerned, as Marx pointed out, are food and sex. In a race where the struggle for existence is a difficult one, food dominates sex ; in civilisation, where the struggle for food, as regards a big proportion of the people, is no longer anything to worry about, sex dominates food. The tendency in modern luxurious life, where every decade the standard of living becomes higher, is towards a sex-dominated age, as in England and America to-day. In such circumstances, where more and more are men and women brought into intimate and disturbing contacts, where sex-appeal is a cultivated feminine art, continence becomes increasingly more difficult. The evil effects of continence are not due to continence *per se*, but to the forcing of continence upon a sexually stimulated nation.

CHAPTER IV

REASONS WHICH LEAD WOMEN TO BECOME PROSTITUTES

It is a popular assumption, based upon the statements of Salvation Army officials, secretaries of societies for reclaiming fallen women, *et al*, that prostitutes are driven into their life of shame through sheer inability to secure work of a respectable nature.

The reasons for the persistence of this assumption are many. For one thing, modern writers of tracts on prostitution, are misled by old and obsolete authorities, such, for instance, as Parent-Duchâtelet, who says " lack of work and insufficient wages are the main causes of prostitution " ; by Sanger, who considers that practically all prostitutes are the " poor victims of circumstances," and would reform if they were given the chance ; and by Sherwell, who, speaking specifically of prostitution in England, says " morals fluctuate with trade."

Now the conditions which applied fifty years ago do not apply to-day. At that time practically the only respectable occupation open to women was marriage. The alternative was domestic service, a form of work which in those days at any rate carried with it a degree of social obloquy. Thus, for the thousands of women of the working-classes who were not lucky enough to get married, the only alternative to domestic service, as regards the huge majority, was to go on the streets. The reports of servant girls who had been seduced and found it impossible to secure re-engagements, in many cases formed the basis of these stories of girls driven to a life of shame to avoid starvation. But even so, it would appear that, from their own researches, these old writers missed the true significance of the enormous proportion of street walkers who had come from the ranks of domestic servants.* Not all of these, by any means, could possibly have been seduced, or have lost their situations through causes which prevented re-engagement. It should have been obvious that a considerable proportion deliberately left service to become ladies of joy.

But however debateable this point may be as regards the past, to-day it admits of no debate whatever. No girl is driven into a life of prostitution through inability to secure a job. There is a bigger demand for domestic servants than there is a supply. Nor will the contention that through some slight moral lapse a girl is unable to secure further work hold water any longer. Through the change in the attitude towards moral peccadillos, the mother of an illegitimate child is no longer

* Sanger found that out of 2,000 New York prostitutes, 933 had formerly been in service. Other writers similarly affirm that the vast majority of prostitutes are recruited from the servant class. Merrick, during his chaplainship of Millbank Prison, found that no less than 53 per cent. of the prostitutes he had to deal with had been servants ; while Sherwell stated that the Salvation Army's register showed that 88 per cent. started life in domestic service. More recently (1916) the anonymous authors of *Downward Paths* give domestic service as the previous occupation of 293 out of 830 prostitutes, and state : " the overwhelming preponderance of domestic servants is in agreement with all other statistics that we have seen."

shunned ; through the universality of contraceptive knowledge and the availability of birth control appliances, there has been a strikingly noticeable decline in the number of pregnancies outside marriage. In view of all these facts it is remarkable that any competent student of sociology should continue to give poverty or lack of work as the main cause of prostitution to-day.

The investigations of vice crusaders and moralists are rarely of much value and often they are dangerously misleading. This statement implies no slur upon the accuracy and sincerity of these investigators—it is merely that they themselves obtain in many cases an inaccurate or only partially true idea through the fact that their investigations are necessarily restricted to certain specialised ranks of prostitutes, and the additional fact that they are very often deliberately misled by the prostitutes themselves.

It is easy to see how this comes about. The social crusader comes into contact with the lowest prostitutes only, usually those who frequent the slums of big cities, and often those who are in prison, in hospital, or are driven through starvation or ill-health to seek help from the various religious or reformative organisations. Now, it is a fact that rarely can a prostitute, *in any circumstances*, be induced to tell the truth as to why she took up her profession. In these special circumstances to which I am alluding, where she is desirous of securing help or eliciting sympathy *she never tells the truth. Any experienced prostitute knows that the surest way to alienate sympathy and interest is to admit that she deliberately chose her profession.*

All of which does not mean that the underlying cause is not economic. It is. It is economic in the sense that dissatisfaction with their position leads most girls to embark upon the career of the prostitute. The servant girl is not satisfied. She wants smart clothes, she wants gaiety, and when circumstances offer her a chance to secure fine clothes and to taste gaiety, she jumps at the opportunity with both feet. It is this dissatisfaction which impels servant girls, in such preponderating numbers, to become prostitutes. Relatively few can ever hope, by sticking to their work, to achieve anything in the way of social or financial success. They may marry policemen or grooms ; they may, failing marriage, become housekeepers ; they may, after years of saving and scraping, be able to open rooming-houses or the like. But for them are none of the possibilities of social climbing which often induce the typist or school-teacher to be content with her lot—the prospect, everlastingly dangling before ambitious eyes, of marrying her employer ; the opportunities for philandering with those who are her social superiors. So, the servant girl itches to escape her destiny. And that peculiar outlook which for some queer reason, associates opprobrium and ignominy with domestic service, is largely to blame for this persistent urge to escape.

Shop-girls, factory workers, in fact all employees in the lower-paid and more servile walks of life are eager to grasp any opportunity to get away from their environment.

Poverty is not a matter that can be defined

ecumenically. What to one person is poverty, to another is comparative wealth. Nor can it be measured solely in terms of money. There are conditions of employment which, to some girls, are not nearly so endurable as prostitution. There are conditions of marriage which involve mental cruelty and degradation such as the successful harlot may never know.

So ! These girls flock to vice like moths flock to the candle. They do not, in many cases, look upon the profession of the prostitute as anything very bad or degrading. They do not look upon it as a sin. If anyone doubts this let them offer to a *successful* prostitute a respectable job such as that of domestic servant or charwoman. The odds are she will either spit in the proposer's face or use language that, even in these days, is quite unprintable.

Let me instance the case of Flossie. Flossie was a typical London street girl. She was on the Wardour Street beat, and, being both young and pretty, she did fairly well. " Why should I give up the profesh. for any job *I* could get," she once said. " A skivvy ! Not on *your* life," she snorted. " My mother was one before she married dad. The boss where she worked got 'er in the family way, and gave dad ten quid to marry 'er. And talkin' of marriage, I'd sooner walk the streets till I dropped than 'ave to go through what mother did. Eight kids besides me. And if she adn't taken the poker to 'im there'd been more—use'd to keep it in bed with 'er ready, she did. O didn't she 'ave a time. I *can* do a bit o' pickin' and choosin'."

A quite different type was a Chicago prostitute

known as " The Countess." She was never
referred to by any other name. You would never
find her on the streets, but she frequented the
smartest of restaurants and night clubs, and was
always beautifully dressed. " I chose my profession
with my eyes wide open, and I've not the slightest
intention of doing anything else until I've made my
pile and can retire, unless, of course, some wealthy
client marries me. What else is there I could do ?
A job "—she spread elegant slender bejewelled
hands—" I was brought up to look pretty and
behave nicely—I never learnt anything else. I've
got a nice bit saved and I might of course go into
business, but it seems to me too risky for this child.
I've not forgotten my friend Sadie putting all
she'd got into a swell restaurant—she lasted just
six months—now she's back where she started.
No sir, I think I'll stick to this safe, conservative,
and very old profession."

As regards ninety-five per cent. of the prostitutes
in this or any other civilised country, the profession
is deliberately chosen. It may, and it is, chosen for
a variety of reasons, and often through the influence
of environmental factors, but it is chosen in preference to other forms of occupation which are
available. So that, in strict truth, as regards the
huge majority, what it is customary to call *causes*
of prostitution are rather *reasons* for the taking up
of the profession of prostitute.

These reasons are many. One cannot point a
finger at any particular one and say this is the sole
reason for girls going on the streets. One cannot
fix upon a certain social failing which should be

remedied or a certain reform which should be instituted, and say this is the solution of the whole difficulty.

Generally speaking, however, the main reasons which induce girls to take to the streets are love of luxury and idleness. Often the two are combined. The one breeds the other to such an extent that it becomes difficult to separate them. The love of "fine and fashionable clothes" is strongly developed in every normal girl, and in many cases the loss of virtue seems to her a small enough price to pay for the realisation of this ambition. In most cases she pays the price. In ever-increasing numbers girls are willing to buy their way to ease, position and fame, through the sale of their bodies. Shopgirls, typists, secretaries, mannequins, chorus girls, domestic servants, and a host of others working at plebeian jobs, who possess any pretence to prettiness, experience the smallest difficulty in finding men who are willing to give them money, to take them out, and to buy them clothes, in exchange for the surrender of what, through the facile morals and precocious sophistication of the day, is becoming of decreasing value. A girl may jib at the idea for a while but, sooner or later, with examples for the finding on every hand, she surrenders.

For truth to tell, in many cases, they place, these girls, few obstacles in the path of their seducers. They are usually delighted to have the opportunity to be taken out to dinner, to a show, and to have a good time generally. Chorus girls and actresses are notorious for their free and easy morals, and many of them are indistinguishable from professional prostitutes in all but name. Some, indeed, are prostitutes who work on the stage without payment because of the opportunities afforded to get in touch with wealthy clients. Others find they must part with their virginity to get any chance at all of climbing towards the stardom which they so feverishly seek.

The first step taken, the rest is easy. The girl becomes what is best described as an amateur prostitute. It is easy to see how from this she gradually drifts into full-time prostitution. The life is comparatively easy, there is no drudgery of work attached to it, and in its initial stages, at any rate, once the step has been taken, it is not without its glamour. There is no disputing the fact that the successful prostitute is well-dressed. In fact, she is better dressed by far than fifty per cent. of other women. There is, further, no disputing the . fact that the higher-class prostitute comes into contact with men in a far better social position than she could ever have hoped to meet had she continued in the walk of life in which God or circumstance had placed her.

It is all very well and good for the woman moving in expensive circles, whose parents are wealthy, or who is married to a millionaire husband, to express amazement at any girl chosing so degrading a profession as that of a harlot, and to argue that she must have been forced into it by poverty or by seduction. It is all very well and good for the raddled and dour Puritan, who is so ugly or so unattractive that the most gorgeous upholstery would serve to intensify rather than to camouflage her shortcomings, to express similar amazement. But neither the one nor the other knows anything about the reasons which induce the girl of poor parentage to look with envy on the successful *fille de joie*. Born of parents and in an environment which hold out the faintest hope of anything beyond a job in a factory or as a domestic servant, with the ultimate hope of marrying a working man ; the vision of the stylish garb of dozens of her kind who have taken to the streets is sufficient to make her long to do the same. There are girls in the slums of London who look upon the profession of the prostitute as something to aspire to and to long for. There are girls by the hundred who consider that the role of professional harlot is no more degrading, sinful or immoral than the role of wife or mistress.

As regards the slum women found in London and in all big cities, this viewpoint is nothing new. It has always been prevalent. The children are brought up in circumstances where there is no mystery attached to the sexual parts or even to the sexual act itself. Promiscuity is thought little of. The overcrowding which, even in these civilised days, is rife in every town, causes whole families to sleep in one bedchamber, and girls and boys are brought up to see the sexual act committed by their parents. Brothers take liberties with their sisters, mutual masturbation is common, incestuous relations are often the inevitable aftermath.* And in the country villages conditions are every bit as bad.

* The author of *The Prevention of Destitution* (London, 1912), says that among the slum children " to have a baby by your father is laughed at as a comic mishap."

The sexual sophistication of country-bred youngsters who are familiar with the sexual intimacies of animals, often far exceeds that of their city brethren. Little wonder that girls reared in such circumstances commit sexual misconduct at an early age, and often drift to the life of the streets as a matter of course.   Moreover, in such an atmosphere, there is inculcated neither respect nor admiration for marriage.   To the decided contrary, the sight of quarrels, of poverty, of drudgery, of beatings, is well calculated to make children look upon prostitution as infinitely preferable to marriage.   The meretricious finery of even the lower-class harlot stands out prominently from the shabby drabness of nine-tenths of married women.   In many cases the mother is a prostitute herself, the father is a pimp, and they send their daughter on the streets without the slightest compunction, often themselves initiating her in sexual intercourse.

In their own primitive way these girls of the slums have grasped the fact which Marro (quoted by Ellis) observes : " The actual conditions of society are opposed to any high moral feeling in women, for between those who sell themselves to prostitution and those who sell themselves to marriage, the only difference is in price and duration of the contract."   Both in marriage and in prostitution, sex is the bait which woman offers to man.   Sex represents the basis of her bargaining. In the case of marriage she holds out for a life-long partnership or its economic equivalent ; in the case of prostitution she accepts a price varying according to circumstances and in all cases representing the best bargain she is able to make for a temporary sexual association.

There are circumstances, too, where even women of gentle birth will choose prostitution as a profession. They may, through circumstances over which they have no control whatever, be compelled to choose between prostitution and suicide or death from starvation. After the Bolshevik revolution, many starving and destitute Russian refugees had to make just this choice. They were on foreign soil, they knew nothing of the language, they were neither trained nor fitted for work of any kind. Naturally, inevitably, in sheer despair, they elected to sell that which finds a ready market wherever men forgather.

Much conflict of opinion exists as to how far sex itself enters into the choice of the profession of prostitute. Morasso says that sexual desire constitutes the main causative factor, and would have us believe that the majority of prostitutes are nymphomaniacal or something not very far removed from it. At the other extreme is Lombroso, who asserts that prostitutes are frigid ; and Maverick, writing in specific reference to London prostitutes, backs up Lombroso's assertion. On the whole, the majority of investigators incline to the view that sensuality is often a predisposing factor in the choice of prostitution as a profession ; and this, too, is the view held by the public, strengthened by the evidence of men who have associated with professional harlots.

In very many cases, however, a simulated sensuality or show of passion may well be mistaken

D

for real sensuality or passion. It should never be forgotten that sex is the prostitute's trade ; that she has all the tricks of this trade at her finger ends. The simulation of passion and more still, of lust, in the shape of exciting the sexual passion of her partner by gratifying his needs or requirements in ways from which a woman of respectability would shrink even if she had any knowledge of their technique, and sometimes to the extent of indulging in perverse practices, have again had a lot to do with the reputation for gross sensuality which the professional harlot has earned for herself. The client of the prostitute, himself gorged with lust, somewhat naturally credits his partner with similar feelings to his own.

It is doubtful, therefore, if prostitutes, *in the main*, at the time of selecting their career, are more sexual than are their respectable sisters. It is, of course, exceedingly difficult to secure any evidence on the point worth the name. It is futile to ask the prostitutes themselves.

It is equally doubtful if they are more frigid than are females in any other class of society. Statements upon which any observations respecting the frigidity of prostitutes are based are almost wholly drawn from *old harlots*, and because of this, if for no other reason, are of amazingly little value. For while there is conceivably room for doubt as to the sensuality or lack of it in young and successful practitioners, in the case of old and unsuccessful ones, there is little room for doubt. The old harlot is invariably frigid. She becomes frigid as she plies her profession. There is abundant evidence of this in the universality of masturbation among prostitutes and in the commonness of homosexualism. The woman who gets pleasure from normal coitus seldom masturbates, and even more seldom is she addicted to homosexualism. It is the lack of pleasure associated with coitus which on the one hand induces and develops masturbatory practices as a means of satisfying sexual desire ; and which on the other hand turns her against intercourse with the opposite sex outside her work, and often leads to the development of homosexual tendencies. The argument that she may have been a homosexual before she became a prostitute will not hold water. It is rare to a degree for a homosexual woman to take up professional prostitution apart from tribadism. But, to the contrary, prostitution is a potent factor in the devlopment of homosexualism and in the fostering of pervert practices. In this connection Moll's assertion that Lesbianism is common among Berlin prostitutes— no less than twenty-five per cent. of them being addicted to its practice—is worthy of note.

If nymphomania were more general it would be a predisposing cause of prostitution of some significance. But nymphomania, though admittedly much more common than in previous ages, is not general enough to affect more than a small proportion of those who become professional harlots. 1955220

At one time it did most assuredly lead a woman to become a prostitute. In Ancient Rome there were ladies of gentle birth who became registered as public prostitutes in order to obtain satisfaction for their sexual passions and appetites. Others had slaves for the express purpose of providing them with sexual pleasure. But in these days of female emancipation, a nymphomaniac has opportunities for indulging, under the guise of respectability, in her passion for venery, that were unavailable to women of other generations. The modern girl who is allowed to go for unchaperoned " car-rides," " week-end jaunts " and " holiday expeditions," with a procession of young men, is in an entirely different position from that of the guarded maiden of a quarter of a century ago.

Apart from those among the poorest classes who prefer to turn a natural inclination into a profession ; it is from the ranks of these better-class girls that are recruited the few nymphomaniacs who today become temporary or permanent prostitutes. The *fille de joie* who has had the advantage of education and culture is not so rare a phenomenon as most people appear to imagine. Hirschfeld says that " more than one woman of good social standing consults me in the course of a year whose daughter has fallen to prostitution."*

The force of example is a factor not to be over-looked, especially in these days when parents more and more exhibit a tendency to allow their daughters to leave home and live in rooms. Undoubtedly it leads to a certain number of such girls taking up prostitution as a part-time or whole-time profession. A girl happens to secure lodgings in the same building as an amateur prostitute and makes her acquaintance ; or, quite unknowingly, she is led

* Magnus Hirschfeld, *Sexual Pathology* : *Being a Study of the Abnormalities of the Sexual Function*, Julian Press, Newark, 1932, p. 147.

to share a room or a flat with one. The sequel, often enough, is that in a relatively short time there are two amateur prostitutes where before there was only one.

Undoubtedly, too, the sharing of apartments or rooms is not without its dangers. It *may possibly* lead to a form of promiscuity which is usually ignored or overlooked in any consideration of prostitution, to wit, female homosexualism or Lesbianism. It is quite impossible to make any kind of an estimate respecting the extent of female homosexualism in this or any other country. The practice of girls living together is so common that it is rare for the possibility of anything evil resulting to be in any way connected with it. And there are no references, veiled or unveiled, in reports of police court cases, to Lesbianism, which, even to the extent of indulgence in overt practices, is not a criminal offence. While, it is true, most of these homosexual alliances are foolish rather than harmful, going little beyond kissing and cuddling, there is always the risk of degeneration into perversity, especially where the professional element enters into it. Where true tribadism is concerned, perverse practices are common, ranging from mutual masturbation and cunnilingus to the use of the mechanical device, referred to variously as *godemiche*, dildoe, *consolateur*, *bijou indiscret*, baubon, and *penis succedaneus*, which would appear to have been employed by savage as well as civilised races in all parts of the world. Among the earliest references to its use are those in the *Mimes of Herondas*, in the *Lysistrata* of Aristophanes, and in the Bible.

CHAPTER V

REASONS WHY MEN SUPPORT PROSTITUTION

THE men who have recourse to prostitutes to satisfy their sexual appetites are both single and married, young and old.

It may be taken as axiomatic that the average man patronises prostitutes through sheer necessity only. In other words, he seeks solace with a prostitute when no other woman, capable or willing to satisfy his wants, is available. With exceptions so few as to be negligible, men are well aware of all the disadvantages and risks attendant on intercourse with street women. In fact, the tendency, if anything, is for these risks to be exaggerated.

In the first place, nine men out of ten are in dread fear of contracting a venereal infection ; in the second place, to the huge majority, the patronage of a prostitute represents a costly affair which can be indulged in at lengthy intervals only ; in the third place, many men, after spending a night with a harlot, have a certain amount of disgust with themselves and are not too anxious that their escapade should be made public property. For all these reasons in general, and occasionally for some other additional reason in particular, it may be taken for granted that the prostitute is the last resource.

We have seen that the basic underlying cause of prostitution is the biological fact that man calls for sexual intercourse almost as universally and as regularly as he calls for food and the other necessaries of life. Admitting the male appetite for sexual intercourse, modern observers and moralists contend that if man could be induced to marry at an earlier age the death-knell of prostitution would be sounded ; that if man could be provided with the safe, legal and inexpensive means of satisfying the demands of his sexual appetite, which means marriage provides, he would cease to patronise the prostitute.

Marriage and prostitution are inextricably interlinked. Every bond which makes the monogamous marriage system more secure coincidentally extends promiscuity in the form of prostitution, free love or adultery. It is the realisation of all this that has led the clergy and the moralists either to lament the necessity for prostitution or to wink at its indulgence. The early Christians realised the impossibility of having one without the other. Thus the efforts of Saint Augustine, of Cato and of Aquinas to justify it, to which reference has already been made. In more recent years Liguori and others have expressed similar views. So, too, the philosophers and thinkers. These views then, expressed or unexpressed, may be taken to be behind the male attitude towards prostitution ; rammed home by the fact that the male justifies his need of sex experience by expressing the view, whether he believes it or not, that coitus is essential to every man as a means of preserving his health. It is the biological justification of his support of the prostitute.

These arguments are based upon an inadequate knowledge of sex and its problems. Their falsity is amply demonstrated by the fact that married men as well as single men patronize prostitutes. Indeed, there are firm grounds for the assumption that married men provide, if not the bulk, certainly the more remunerative section, of the harlot's clientele.

The motive which drives a man into the arms of a prostitute in preference or in addition to those of his wife may be any one of a dozen conceivable reasons. In the first place there are the preponderating number of men, especially single men unversed in the mysteries of sex, and married men whose sexual adventures are limited to the woman they have married, whose sexual appetites, once they have been thoroughly aroused, cannot be satiated by any one respectable woman, and who subscribe too literally to the doctrine, propounded with Rabelaisian humour by Benjamin Franklin, that all women are alike in the dark. The Franklin document* is of such interest that I cannot refrain from reproducing it here.

* This letter, which was written in 1745 to some correspondent whose name, if known, has never been disclosed, and was probably intended for reading to a select circle of cronies, much as Robert Burns was accustomed to read his collection of salacious verse known as *The Merry Muses*, was discovered years after Franklin's death in an accumulation of documents and correspondence. It was eventually purchased, along with many other manuscripts, by the United States Government. This particular document, known as *A Letter to a Young Man on the Choice of a Mistress*, the existence of which had long been known to a few, was rigidly suppressed until comparatively recently, and gained for itself a notoriety equal to that associated with the satirical Franklin document entitled *A Letter on Perfumes to the Academy of Brussels*. Except for the substitution of the modern " s " where the obsolete character used by Franklin appeared, this is a transcription of the original document.

Philadelphia, 1745.

To My Dear Friend,

I know of no medicine fit to diminish the violent natural inclinations you mention ; and if I did, I think I should not communicate it to you. Marriage is the proper remedy.*   It is the most natural State of man, and therefore the State in which you are most likely to find solid Happiness. Your reasons against entering into it at present appear to me not well founded. The circumstantial advantages you have in view by postponing it, are not only uncertain, but they are small in comparison with that of the Thing itself, the being married and settled. It is the Man and Woman united that make the complete human being. Separate, She wants his Force of Body and Strength of Reason ; he, her Softness, Sensibility and acute Discernment. Together they are more likely to succeed in the World. A single man has not nearly the value he would have in the State of Union. He is an incomplete Animal. He resembles the odd half of a pair of Scissors. If you get a prudent, healthy Wife, your Industry in your Profession, with her good Economy, will be a fortune sufficient.

But if you will not take this Counsel and persist in thinking a Commerce with the Sex inevitable, then I repeat my former Advice, that in all your Amours you should prefer old Women to young ones.

---

* It is a noteworthy and an interesting point that Benjamin Franklin subscribed to Saint Paul's dictum that " it is better to marry than to burn."

You call this a Paradox and demand my Reasons. They are these :

1. Because they have more Knowledge of the World, and their Minds are better stored with Observations, their Conversation is more improving, and more lastingly agreeable.

2. Because when Women cease to be handsome they study to be good. To maintain their Influence over men, they supply the Diminution of Beauty by an Augmentation of Utility. They learn to do a thousand Services small and great, and are the most tender and useful of Friends when you are sick. Thus they continue amiable. And hence there is hardly such a thing to be found as an old Woman who is not a good Woman.

3. Because there is no Hazard of Children, which irregularly produced may be attended with much Inconvenience.

4. Because through more Experience they are more prudent and discreet in conducting an Intrigue to prevent Suspicion. The Commerce with them is therefore safer with regard to your Reputation. And with regard to theirs, if the Affair should happen to be known, considerate People might be rather inclined to excuse an old Woman, who would kindly take care of a young man, form his Manners by her good counsels, and prevent his ruining his Health and Fortune among mercenary Prostitutes.

5. Because in every Animal that walks upright, the Deficiency of the Fluids that fill the muscles appears first in the highest Part. The

Face first grows lank and wrinkled ; then the Neck ; then the Breast and Arms ; the lower Parts continuing to the last as plump as ever ; so that covering all above with a Basket, and regarding only what is below the Girdle, it is impossible of two Women to know an old one from a young one. And as in the dark all Cats are grey, the Pleasure of Corporal Enjoyment with an old Woman is at least equal, and frequently superior; every Knack being, by Practice, capable of Improvement.

6. Because the Sin is less. The debauching a Virgin may be her Ruin, and make her for life unhappy.

7. Because the Compunction is less. The having made a young girl miserable may give you frequent bitter Reflections ; none of which can attend the making of an old Woman happy.

8. And lastly, They are so grateful !

This much for my paradox. But still I advise you to marry directly, being sincerely.

Your affectionate Friend,

BENJAMIN FRANKLIN.

Now, like most of the facile aphorisms expressed by sophisticated rodomontadists, amateur Casanovas, smart-alecks, and merchants of bravura, the notion that all women are alike in respect of their capacity for giving sexual satisfaction to men, is a fallacy. The error is due to the cynical vaporizings of those who are blind to the psychological factors affecting sexual intercourse on the one hand, and the great variations in the technique of coitus and its connotations on the other. Where the pleasure connected with sex is a purely physical pleasure, coitus is, at best, a poor affair, and is little removed from a masturbatory process. It is in such a case that the personality and appearance of the woman count for nothing—the man is so oblivious to female charm and individuality, that he would very nearly experience the same degree of sexual satisfaction with a cadaver.

Most men, however, of any intelligence or culture find that the charm, beauty and personality of the woman, produce physical repercussions which in turn have considerable effect upon the satisfaction and pleasure resulting from the sex act itself. And most men, too, find that a woman versed in the technique of coitus and its variations, is quite unlike one who is as ignorant of this technique as she is indifferent. Even if the man himself is in possession of the requisite knowledge, he rarely cares, in such circumstances, to adopt the role of instructor. Certainly if the woman were his wife, he would shrink from such a task. With a prostitute the matter is on an entirely different footing. It is rarely necessary for the man to do any suggesting. The woman herself adopts the role of teacher. A mastery of the technique of both normal and abnormal methods of coitus is part of her job.

Even apart from the call for bizarre methods of intercourse, the prostitute, in a very large number of cases, can arouse the sexual passion of the man where his wife completely fails. It is not alone the allure of a strange woman, which invariably possesses some power as an aphrodisiac ; but partly is it due to the mastery of the knack of arousing sensual thoughts

that the harlot undoubtedly possesses. Her mode
of dress, her manner, her conversation : all are
deliberately designed to one end. The result is
that mere propinquity to a prostitute will often
arouse in a married man a degree of sexual desire
that, after the honeymoon weeks, he rarely experiences when in the company of his wife.

It is due to all these reasons that there are married
men, and they are not few in number, who, while
they have the highest degree of reverence and
respect for their wives, are yet so little aroused
sexually in their presence that they seldom experience the slightest desire for sexual intercourse with
them ; yet in the company of other women these
same men are goaded almost beyond endurance.
Men of this type, who are married to women of
charm, culture and beauty, and yet regularly
consort with prostitutes, are a puzzle to their
friends and acquaintances unversed in the problems
and subtleries of sexual psychology.

Then again, it must be remembered that beauty
is not of the faintest value as an indication of sexual
appetite or capacity. There are women rivalling
the most beautiful film stars in appearance who
prove to have no more sexual passion than a
eunuch. The men they marry find this out only
after marriage.

Old men are frequent clients of prostitutes. In
addition to the fact that all ordinary methods of
arousing sexual passion have long since ceased to
produce the slightest effect, and only abnormal
methods of stimulation will induce the desired
results ; most sensual old men have a penchant for

young and pretty females. Their wives no longer possess the faintest attraction for them sexually.

There is, too, a widespread belief in the revitalizing and rejuvenating power which coitus with a young girl, and especially a virgin, possesses for an old man. It is based upon the theory that some vital fluid is absorbed during the act of intercourse. Students of the Bible will recall that David performed the sexual act with the young Abisag for this very purpose.

Finally, there are the sexual perverts, old and young, married and single, who are regular clients of prostitutes. They constitute, these sexual perverts, a far larger proportion of men than most people have any conception of. There are the fetichists, who can only perform the sexual act in certain circumstances or in special surroundings. There are brothels in Paris and other Continental cities where such men are accommodated. Tarnowsky, the Russian sexologist, quotes the case mentioned in Taxil's *La Prostitution contemporaine,* where a special apartment in a Parisian brothel was draped in black satin, with silver ornamentation, and a prostitute, laid full length upon a bed, her face and body whitened, played the role of a corpse. When all was ready, " a prelate in sacerdotal vestments " entered, knelt at the side of the bed, and after murmuring something reminiscent of a mass for the dead, hurled himself upon the motionless and silent prostitute.

These and other elaborate arrangements for satisfying the whims of wealthy perverts are features of the more expensive houses of prostitution. Thus

Taxil mentions the frequency with which, in Parisian brothels, perverts known as " *stercoraires*," are provided with vulgar and disgusting exhibitions connected with the evacuative processes. In the case of a pervert of this particular class only such a spectacle is sufficient to induce a degree of sexual excitement which will bring on an erection.

Men who, through age, long-continued masturbation, excessive coitus, or other causes, are temporarily or permanently stricken with impotence, in the brothels, find companions who will allow them to wear mechanical devices for overcoming their disability—devices from the employment of which their wives would shrink in disgust. In fact, few men would care to suggest to any respectable woman the adoption of such measures. Many of the impotent men, too, are supplied with the necessary instruments and given instructions in their proper use, by the brothel inmates. Among the best known of these devices are the rings, constructed of gold, silver, celluloid or rubber, which are fixed around the *corona glandis* ; india-rubber rings which clasp tightly the base of the penis and thus enable erections to last longer ; spiked and corrugated condoms ; and an instrument mentioned by Kisch,* known as the " *schlitten*," which is designed to make possible the introduction into the vagina of the impotent man's semi-flaccid penis.

Prostitutes living in single rooms or in small flats rarely are able to provide anything so elaborate as is possible in the brothels. And there are other

* E. Heinrich Kisch, *The Sexual Life of Woman*, 1910.

difficulties in the way. But there are plenty of London prostitutes who have whips and other articles of punishment in their rooms for use with the numerous sadists and masochists who patronise them.

PART II

HISTORY OF PROSTITUTION

CHAPTER VI

PROSTITUTION AMONG SAVAGE AND
PRIMITIVE RACES

PROSTITUTION in the present-day legal sense of the term is a sore of civilisation. Strictly speaking, it has never existed among savage races in the sense that we know the professional prostitution of Leicester Square or the Montmartre or the Bowery. From this it is easy to make the facile assumption that savages are more chaste and more moral than civilised men and women. It is a contention that is often brought forward by writers on anthropology and ethnology. The lack of prostitution is looked upon as evidence of a lack of promiscuous intercourse, and as a proof of greater chastity among savages. Actually it presents no such evidence.

The connotation between absence of prostitution and existence of chastity is due to the failure to realise that in most savage races there exists a degree of promiscuity which in all but legal definition is indistinguishable from prostitution itself. When the whole available female population of a country acts like a professional harlot does in other countries, there is and there can be no such thing as professional prostitution.

To understand the position clearly, it must be kept in mind that the existence of prostitution depends upon the coincidental existence of one of two things : (1) the property right in virginity ; or (2) the presence of some form of marriage.

In many savage tribes virginity is thought little of ; in others it is thought nothing of. And, in certain cases, its existence after the coming of puberty constitutes a definite handicap, if not a disgrace. Marco Polo says that among the Tibetans no man would " on any consideration take to wife a girl who was a maid ; for they say a wife is nothing worth unless she has been used to consort with men." According to Westermarck, among the Akamba tribe in British East Africa, a pregnant girl is regarded as " a most eligible spouse " ; and in the Mongwandis of the Upper Mongala and the Bagas of French Guinea, men intending marriage prefer for their wives girls who have already given birth to children.* Among many savage races in different parts of the world, the very fact of a woman having been the lover of many men is a great asset to her in securing a husband. The man who marries such a woman looks upon her as a most desirable creature seeing that she has attracted the attentions of so many other men.

Marriage in the civilised sense has always been preceded by communal marriage or polyandry, where the women of the race or tribe are, for the purpose of sexual intercourse, the common property of the males. Here, there is no individual property right in the woman, and actually this communal marriage is almost equivalent to what, in more

* Edward Westermarck, *The History of Human Marriage*, fifth edition, Vol. I (Macmillan).

civilised states, is termed prostitution. According to Theopompus " among the Tyrrhenians, it was a law that the women were common property."

With the coming into existence of any form of monogamous union, prostitution is an inevitable aftermath. The polygamous nature of man on the one hand and the surplusage of women on the other, render it, as we have seen, a universal concomitant.

Among certain tribes of the Indians of North America, marriage, if such it can be called, was little different from promiscuity. Many a maiden, when it became sufficiently obvious that any prospects of marriage were remote, and a suitable opportunity presented itself, such as a feast or other assembly, would invite the bucks of the tribe in turn to have intercourse with her. So far from this practice causing the girl to be despised by those wishing to marry, it usually induced one of them to ask her to be his wife.

In many parts of Africa, notably in Dahomey, the custom whereby the king has the right to have intercourse with every woman, is really a form of prostitution. Concubines are common, and chiefs, medicine men and other highly placed dignatories have the right to take as many wives or concubines as they think fit. Women are bought and discarded at a moment's notice, and the majority of these become harlots in every sense of the term, selling their sexual charms to all comers.

Much of the promiscuity among savage and semi-civilised races is developed into actual prostitution by the traders, sailors and even the missionaries who come into contact with the natives. From accounts, by travellers and explorers, of life in various remote parts of the world, it is evident that European sailors, traders and missionaries were accustomed to hire native women to become their " temporary wives." Neither the women themselves nor their parents or husbands saw anything degrading in these promiscuous associations with foreign men. It was undoubtedly in this way that commercial prostitution and brothels came to be established in many savage or semi-civilised countries. Mayhew and Hemyng, in *London Labour and London Poor*, dealing with prostitution among the Maories of New Zealand, and referring to Jerningham Wakefield's description of the arrival of whalers in New Zealand ports, say : " He mentions as one of the most important transactions following this event, the providing of the company with " wives for the season.' Some had regular helpmates, but others were forced to hire women. Bargains were formally struck, and when a woman failed to give satisfaction, she was exchanged for another."* The same writers mention that " In the criminal calendar of Wellington for 1846, we find one native convicted and punished for keeping a house of ill-fame."**

As money or its equivalent enters into the thing, prostitution tends to develop. In all countries and in all races, there are for the finding parents who are perfectly willing to prostitute their daughters for money, and the daughters themselves, as they reach

* Mayhew, *London Labour and London Poor*, Extra volume, Griffith Bohn, 1862, p. 75.

** *Ibid.*, p. 75.

puberty, are in many instances willing to sacrifice their virginity for presents or cash. Westermarck quotes Porter* as saying that the girls of Madison Island (one of the Marquesas group) " are the wives of all who can purchase their favours, and a handsome daughter is considered by her parents as a blessing which secures to them, for a time, wealth and abundance."

Similarly, " among the Line Islanders of the Gilbert Group . . . . a woman was at liberty to accept as many men as would take her, provided they paid for the privilege."** Westermarck also gives instances, culled from the writings of various authorities, of the loaning out for money of their daughters and wives developing into professional harlotry among native races in various parts of the world, notably in the Melanesian Islands, in the Caroline Islands, in Uganda, in Greenland, and among numerous Indian tribes of North, Central and South America.

Many girls, too, either of their own free will or in response to parental instructions, adopted the role of temporary prostitute in order to earn a marriage dowry. Brantôme mentions this custom being prevalent in the olden days among the women of Cyprus, who hied themselves to the shore and earned money from the sailors calling at the island. In Nicaragua, a similar custom was prevalent.

In many primitive and semi-civilised tribes it has been, and it still is, in some cases, customary to

* Porter, *Journal of a Cruise made in the Pacific Ocean.*

** Tutuila, " Line Islanders " in *Journal Polynesian Society*, i., 270, quoted by Westermarck, *The History of Human Marriage.*

select for the specific purpose of providing sexual pleasure, certain women and men. That these individuals are not termed prostitutes does not alter the fact that in everything else except name they are equivalent to the inmates of the more depraved and licentious of the Continental and South American brothels. Thus among the Tanni Islanders of Polynesia, a number of girls are reserved and trained in every form of sexual perversion. Perhaps, however, the most notorious of such practices, was that referred to by Hammond in relation to his study of the Pueblo Indians of New Mexico. In each village it was customary for one young male to be selected for use as a pathic by all the other males. He was termed a *mujerado*, which means literally " changed into a woman."

CHAPTER VII

RELIGIOUS PROSTITUTION

IN its earlier phases prostitution was always associated with religion ; and there seems strong grounds for the assumption that the first brothels were run by priests. But instead of being called brothels, they were described as temples, and their inmates, instead of being dubbed prostitutes, were referred to as daughters of the temple, priestesses of Venus, or in other euphemised terms.

The origin of religious prostitution has been the subject of much speculation and various hypotheses have been formulated to account for it. Many early anthropologists looked upon it as a form of fertility cult, arguing that the promiscuous unions of men and women at certain festivals were thought to have marked effects upon, and to be essential to, the fertility of animals and the productiveness of the land. With the coming of monogamous marriage and the consequent decline of promiscuity, it became necessary to segregate a certain proportion of the female population for these essential fertility cults. These women, who sacrificed their virginity and their right to marriage, were looked upon much in the way that we today are accustomed to look upon nuns and priests who, in the service of God, eschew all rights to the sexual pleasures and amenities of normal life.

This fertility-rite hypothesis, however, though conceivably it may have applied in certain instances, is much too narrow to serve as a universal explanation of the origin of religious or sacred prostitution. It certainly can have had no connection with the origin of male prostitution which, in those early days, was as widespread and as intimately connected with religion as was female prostitution.

There would seem to be far stronger ground for assuming that religious prostitution was an outcome of the beliefs, common to almost every ancient race, that sexual intercourse with a god or goddess, or with anyone intimately associated or connected with a god or goddess, was beneficial to the human participator.* This explanation accounts for the practice in some countries of every female assuming, with neither shame nor reluctance, the role of temporary harlot, and of no stigma attaching to this in the eyes of either her female or male compatriots.

Thus, according to Herodotus,** the women of Babylonia were required to sit in the temple of Mylitta until some men claimed the right to have intercourse with them. In other words, each woman was required to become a temporary prostitute, the fee paid by the man constituting an offering to the goddess presiding over the temple. Each woman was required to remain in the temple until some man selected her—the plain and the ugly were often compelled to remain for months and sometimes

* According to Westermarck (*The History of Human Marriage*) : " In Morocco, supernatural benefits are to this day expected not only from heterosexual but also from homosexual intercourse with a holy person."
** Herodotus, Book I, Ch. CXCIX.

years on end before the act of prostitution released them.   Nor was this any isolated instance—it merely stands out because Herodotus described it in such detail.   There are, it is true, some who affirm that the account of Herodotus is fictitious, but these critics have overlooked the fact that there are for the finding confirmatory statements by contemporary observers.   The scribes responsible for the *Epistle of Jeremy*, which is one of the books of the Apocrypha, say : " It is said that the Babylonian women with cords about them sit in the ways, burning bran for incense ; but if any of them, drawn by some that passeth by, be with him, she reproacheth her fellow, that she was not thought as worthy as herself, nor her cord broken."

Herodotus also refers to a similar temple in Corinth ; Juvenal asserts that the Roman temples were all licensed brothels ; and customs requiring females to act as temporary prostitutes in the service of the goddesses were frequent in many parts of Asia and Africa.   In other instances permanent prostitutes were attached to the temples. Strabo, a contemporary historian, referring to the Temple of Aphrodite Porne at Corinth, says it contained over one hundred *hetairae*, all of whom were required to serve the goddess.   Sumner says that " under the Caesars the most beautiful girl of the noble families of Thebes was chosen to be consecrated in the temple of Ammon. She gained honour and profit by the life of a courtesan, and always found a grand marriage when she retired on account of age."*   The dancing-girls which,

* W. G. Sumner, *Folkways*, Ginn & Co., Boston, 1907, p. 541.

until recently, were openly attached to so many temples in India were prostitutes who had intercourse when required with the priests and other temple officials, and with visitors for payment. For generations it was the custom in many parts of India for every first-born female child to be dedicated to the tribal god, to whom she was supposed to be married, and made to serve as a temple prostitute. How far this and other analogous customs survive today it is almost impossible to discover. Under British rule efforts have been made to stamp out temple prostitution, but there are reasons for believing that it still exists in modified and surreptitious forms. Among some of the Western African tribes, certain girls are not allowed to marry. They are, like the nuns in more civilised countries, dedicated to the service of their god and known as priestesses consecrated to the deity.* In all but name they are prostitutes. As such they serve the priests attached to the tribe ; and in addition, any other men willing to pay for their services, in the form of a gift to the god. According to Westermarck,** certain female members of the Eiwe-speaking tribes of the Slave Coast, who are dedicated to the god, are in reality prostitutes, though this is in no way anything to merit reproach, every act of

* This pagan belief is paralleled by the early Christian dedication of virgins to God and Christ and the belief that the Lord had intercourse with these " consecrated " women (e.g., the Virgin Mary). The only difference is that while the " consecrated '* pagans were prostitutes, the Christian " consecrated " women were the wives of God and Christ. This belief was in accordance with the early Christian concept of celibacy.

** Edward Westermarck, *The Origin and Development of the Moral Ideas.* Macmillan, 1917.

licentiousness of which they are guilty being looked upon as directed by their god. Similarly, on the Gold Coast, the priestesses are forbidden to marry, but may have sexual intercourse with any man they desire, having a right of choice analogous to the *jus primae noctis* exercised in so many countries by kings and priests.

A solitary act of prostitution, where the virgin girl is deflowered by a priest or other holy person representing the god to whom she is offering her virginity, or with a stranger, had its origin in the fear of harm resulting to the man who married a virgin on the occasion of his first sexual intercourse with her. This belief was widespread among ancient races, and to this day is not unknown in certain primitive or savage tribes. It was this almost universal disinclination or fear on the part of the bridegroom to deflower a virgin wife, at any rate by sexual intercourse, that led to the institution of the *jus primae noctis*, that curious and barbarous custom where the defloration of every bride was conceded to be the right of the king, or the chief, or the priest, or the medicine-man, according to the nature of the State or the tribe or the race in question. It is customary for modern observers to look upon the *jus primae noctis* as a cruel right exercised by all-powerful rulers, and strongly resented by those who were compelled to submit to it. This was certainly true in the later years of its survival, But originally, the right was gladly given, and the bridegroom, far from resenting the deflowering of his virgin wife, made every effort to find someone willing to perform the act of

defloration.* That he was misled by the crafty priests
of the day intent upon finding an excuse for the satisfying of their carnal appetites does not affect the
point.   He believed most firmly that harm would
surely come to him if he ruptured the hymen himself ; just as today thousands of persons believe
that any attempt to prevent conception is a sin in
the eyes of God.

There is justification for the assumption that
much of the fear connected with the act of defloration results through the hemorrhage which accom-
panies the rupturing of the hymenal membrane—
a fear analogous to that associated with the menstrual discharge.   For in many cases the blood
resulting from a first coitus, like menstrual blood,
is deemed to be poisonous to ordinary mortals.
Only holy persons, such as the priests of god,
chiefs and kings, could deflower a virgin girl with
impunity.   True, occasionally, foreigners or men of
other tribes, supposedly immune from danger,**
were induced to perform the act of defloration.   In
other instances, they were often paid to run the

---

* In certain cases defloration was accomplished without coitus.   In
Samoa, according to Krama, the bridegroom destroys the hymen with his
forefinger ;   in other instances a stick or a skewer is used ;   in the
Philippines the act of defloration is accomplished by one of the old women
of the tribe ;   in India the stone, ivory, or wooden phallus of an idol or god
is used to rupture the hymen.   A similar custom was prevalent among the
Moabites, the pagan worshippers of Baal-poer, referred to so often in the
Old Testament. The priestesses or prostitutes serving the god Baal had their
hymens ruptured on the stone phalli of the idols which were to be found
in all the temple-brothels.

** Westermarck, in *History of Human Marriage*, and Hartland, in *Ritual
and Belief*, state that in many races a stranger was looked upon as a sort of
semi-supernatural being, on a par with a priest or holy man, with whom
intercourse was not only free from all risk to the man but beneficial to
the woman.

risk—a risk by the way which applied more specifically to the bridegroom, who was supposed to be at
this time in his life peculiarly likely to be the
victim of evil influences.

In certain tribes the *jus primae noctis* becomes an
occasion for what in other and in all civilised races
would be termed incest. The right of defloration
belongs to the father of the virgin girl. Westermarck
gives instances of this custom, quoting the statements of a seventeenth century writer named Her-
fort, that among the Sinhalese it was usual for the
father to deflower his own daughter on the eve of
her marriage, on the ground of " having a right to
the first fruit of the tree he had planted." A similar
custom was observed in certain Malayan tribes.

In other instances where no specific persons are
given the right of defloration, the *jus primae noctis*
is openly offered for sale. Westermarck instances
the custom among the Mfiote, a tribe inhabiting
the coast of Loango, of dressing up girls who have
reached puberty and hawking them round from
village to village. Roth, Spencer and Gillen, and
other authorities, state that in many Australian
tribes each young woman on arrival at puberty, is
carried into the bush and forced to submit to coitus
with a number of young bucks of the tribe. It is a
tribal custom that before any girl becomes the
exclusive property of one man, she must submit,
after the crude initiative laceration of the vagina,
to promiscuous sexual intercourse with a number of
selected males.

It is easy to see that from the sale or grant of the
jus primae noctis, in accordance with tribal laws and

F

superstitious observances, the step towards religious prostitution as a temporary or permanent profession is but a small one. There is a passage in *The Testament of Judah*, in which it is stated that " it was a law of the Amorites that she who was about to marry should sit in fornication seven days by the gate."*

This practice in turn led to the giving of part of their earnings to the temple, possibly to placate the priests, and the retention of part for themselves. In India, in addition to the dancing girls dedicated to a life's servitude to the god of the temple, there were other harlots who retained part of their earnings for themselves.

In any consideration of religious prostitution one must not overlook the fact that, in some cases certainly and in many cases probably, the cloak of religion was used to excuse, justify or camouflage what was nothing but licentiousness of the most shameless brand. It would be difficult indeed to name any form of sexual vice, from promiscuity to perversions of the most loathsome type, that has not, under some euphemized name or other, been sanctioned by and upheld by religion. And this is by no means restricted to ancient pagan or savage forms of religion. The polygamy of the Mormons, the perversions of the Oneida Community, are examples in comparatively recent times and in civilised countries ; the obscene and perverse rites which characterise the devil worshippers of Paris and London are examples in our own day.

---

* *Testaments of the Twelve Patriarchs*, translated by Charles.

CHAPTER VIII

PROSTITUTION IN THE BIBLE

THE Bible, and particularly the Old Testament, contains a good many references to, and a certain amount of information about, prostitution before the advent of Christianity. In the opinion of theologians and moralists it contains too much information, and there are religious teachers, clergymen, and others, who hurriedly turn over certain scandalous pages and omit certain obscene passages when reading from the Sacred Books for the edification of the young and the unsaved. As long ago as the days of Saint Jerome, the young were forbidden to have access to the Book of Ezekiel ; and even today, divorced from their context, I have an idea that the descriptions of the whoredoms of Abolah and Aholibah would be put down by the moralists and Comstockians as rank pornography.

At that particular period with which the Old Testament deals, consorting with prostitutes appears from all the available evidence, to have been looked upon much as in civilised countries it is looked upon today—or perhaps it would be more correct to say that, after all these centuries, apart from the fortuitous spasms of persecution and attempted repression which we shall consider in another chapter, there has been no appreciable alteration in the reaction of society as a whole to prostitution.

Publicly the prostitute was denounced, just as she is today ; privately she was supported and encouraged. Of this denunciation the Bible gives many instances. Thus Solomon denounced her in the following terms :

" My son, keep my words, and lay up my commandments with thee. Keep my commandments, and live ; and my law as the apple of thine eye. Bind them upon thy fingers, write them upon the table of thine heart. Say unto wisdom, Thou art my sister ; and call understanding thy kinswoman : That they may keep thee from the strange woman, from the stranger which flattereth with her words. For at the window of my house I looked through my casement, and beheld among the simple ones, I discerned among the youths, a young man void of understanding, Passing through the street near her corner ; and he went the way to her house, In the twilight, in the evening, in the black and dark night : And, behold, there met him a woman with the attire of an harlot, and subtile of heart. (She is loud and stubborn ; her feet abide not in her house : Now is she without, now in the streets, and lieth in wait at every corner). So she caught him, and kissed him, and with an impudent face said unto him, I have peace-offerings with me ; this day have I paid my vows. Therefore came I forth to meet thee, diligently to seek thy face, and I have found thee. I have decked my bed with coverings of tapestry, with carved works, with fine linen of

Egypt. I have perfumed my bed with myrrh, aloes, and cinnamon. Come, let us take our fill of love until the morning ; let us solace ourselves with loves. For the good man is not at home, he is gone a long journey. He hath taken a bag of money with him, and will come home at the day appointed. With her much fair speech she caused him to yield, with the flattering of her lips she forced him. He goeth after her straightway, as an ox goeth to the slaughter, or as a fool to the correction of the stocks ; Till a dart strike through his liver ; as a bird hasteth to the snare, and knoweth not that it is for his life. Hearken unto me now therefore, O ye children, and attend to the words of my mouth. Let not thine heart decline to her ways, go not astray in her paths. For she hath cast down many wounded : yea, many strong men have been slain by her. Her house is the way to hell, going down to the chambers of death.

And yet Solomon's famous temple, ornamented with phallic symbols, harbouring sodomites and whores, was nothing but a brothel, in which perversions associated with the worship of Baal and Moloch, and so vigorously denounced in the Sacred Books, were surreptitiously practised, and Solomon himself, in common with other Biblical kings, had mistresses and concubines numbering many hundreds. The widow Tamar, in an attempt to secure for herself a husband, assumed the attire of a prostitute.

It was Moses, spokesman for Jehovah, who railed at the idea of prostitution : " Do not prostitute

thy daughter, to cause her to be a whore ; lest the
land fall to whoredom, and the land become full
of wickedness " (Leviticus xix. 29). And again :
" There shall be no whore of the daughters of Israel,
nor a sodomite of the sons of Israel. Thou shalt
not bring the hire of a whore, or the price of a dog,
into the house of the Lord thy God for any vow :
for even both these are abomination unto the Lord
thy God " (Deuteronomy xxiii. 17-18). Yet he
took no actual prohibitory measures against the
cohabitation of young men with prostitutes from
other lands.

Most of the old Hebrew prophets and lawmakers
themselves patronised harlots, and looked upon
such escapades as the mildest of peccadillos. In
instance, the powerful and wealthy Judah, praised
and worshipped by his brethren,* slept with a
harlot** and made no secret of the fact. Jephthah,
the Gileadite,*** who was a judge in Israel for six
years, was the son of a prostitute. In short, promiscuous sexual relations on the part of men, so long
as they were not unduly advertised, came in for
little in the way of censure. But the woman caught
in adultery, or pursuing the profession of the harlot,
was denounced, harassed and punished. It was
the universal attitude of man towards woman
asserting itself. Women, other than his own
relatives, were to be pursued and seduced. Hence,
to preserve as much as possible the chastity of his

* " Judah, thou art he whom thy brethren shall praise : thy hand shall
be in the neck of thine enemies ; thy father's children shall bow down
before thee " (Genesis, xlix. 8).

** Genesis xxxviii. 18.

*** Judges xi. 1.

female adherents, the punishments for adultery or fornication on the part of the married or betrothed woman were enacted ; the harsh stipulation against prostitution within the race ; the command against the employment of prostitutes in the temples.

When we come to consider the many references to male prostitution in the Old Testament we see an entire change of attitude, and the new attitude here expressed has dominated the reaction of society towards sodomy and its analogues in all Christian countries through the ages. We have seen that female prostitutes were attached, under various euphemistic names, to most of the temples throughout the then known world, and that the Hebrew temples were no exceptions. But in certain races, worshipping gods other than Jehovah, male prostitutes also were attached to the temples. The vehemence with which sodomy was denunciated by the Hebrews was due more to the fact that it was a feature of a rival and so-called heretical religion than because of the practice itself. Westermarck has pointed out that " the word *Kādēsh*, translated ' sodomite,' properly denotes a man dedicated to a deity ; and it appears that such men were consecrated to the mother of the gods, the famous Dea Syria, whose priests or devotees they were considered to be."* The sin which, according to the Hebrew ideology, towered above every other sin, was disbelief in the Lord God Jehovah and the worshipping of other gods. The first commandment was essentially the most important. It was natural that the mere fact of

* Edward Westermarck, *The Origin and Development of the Moral Ideas*.

worshippers of rival gods practising sodomy should have led the Hebrews to give to the world this explanation as their justification for a policy of rigorous persecution and oppression. Sodom and Gomorrah were destroyed because they were the seats of heretical cults, of which the practice of unnatural sexual vice was but one feature. Thus connotations between idolatry and sodomy were established, and we see the recurrent denunciation which runs through the Bible :

" Thou shalt not lie with mankind as with womankind : it is abomination " (Leviticus xviii. 22).

" If a man also lie with mankind as he lieth with a woman, both of them have committed an abomination : they shall surely be put to death ; their blood shall be upon them " (Leviticus xx. 13).

" And there were also sodomites in the land, and they did according to all the abominations of the nations which the Lord cast out before the children of Israel " (I Kings xiv. 24).

But I shall have occasion, in another chapter, to examine more closely the question of sodomy and its relation to prostitution.

With the coming of Christianity the sex act, in any form, and whether committed in wedlock or otherwise, was denounced. The dour and ascetic Saint Paul glorified celibacy and chastity until they became prominent features of the early Christian religion. It was this outlook on sex which led to the rule that no man or woman, married or unmarried, who had performed the sex act the previous night should take part in a Church festival or in the Eucharist.

At the same time there was a change from the relentless and sadistic cruelty which was so marked a feature of the Mosaic code ; and the adulterer and the prostitute were no longer hounded to death for their sins. The teaching of Christ was mainly one of forgiveness and charity. We see this well exemplified in his treatment of the harlot :

" And the scribes and Pharisees brought unto him a woman taken in adultery ; and when they had set her in the midst, They say unto him, Master, this woman was taken in adultery, in the very act. Now Moses in the law commanded us, that such should be stoned ; but what sayest thou ? This they said, tempting him, that they might have to accuse him. But Jesus stooped down, and with his finger wrote on the ground, as though he heard them not. So, when they continued asking him, he lifted up himself, and said unto them, He that is without sin among you, let him first cast a stone at her. And again he stooped down, and wrote on the ground. And they which heard it, being convicted by their own conscience, went out one by one, beginning at the eldest, even unto the last : and Jesus was left alone, and the woman standing in the midst. When Jesus had lifted up himself, and saw none but the woman, he said unto her, Woman, where are those thine accusers ? hath no man condemned thee ? She said, No man, Lord. And Jesus said unto her, Neither do I condemn thee : go, and sin no more " (John viii. 3-11).

CHAPTER IX

DEVELOPMENT OF PROSTITUTION
UNDER CIVILISATION

WHEN once religious prostitution had been definitely established it was bound in time to develop into professional prostitution as we know it to-day, and as every country in which monogamous marriage is an institution has known it since the dawn of civilisation. Every step that is made to tighten up monogamy and, coincidentally, to ostracise free love, is bound to develop prostitution. So much so, indeed, that the growth of prostitution inevitably follows the path of the missionary in savage and semi-civilised countries.

We can trace the growth of prostitution step by step. First we have the promiscuity of savages ; next religious or sacred prostitution ; finally professional harlotry, which 'may be either of the free-lance kind or brothel prostitution. Often one form was so intermixed with another, or was carried on under a religious ægis for the sake of appearances, that it is difficult to discover where exactly religious prostitution finished and professional prostitution began. The monetary aspect entered into it, however, whatever may have been the ostensible

; to Herodotus, the Pyra-
ney derived from prostitu-
ar as to drive his own
on in order to build the
ame. Actually, in most
when commandeered by
:o ply their profession in
iblic brothels.

e population of Ancient
full of significance, and
ig attention. Moreover,
:ls, as we shall see later,

in modern civilisation. Women, respectable
women—that is, wives, daughters, and relatives—
were looked upon as so many pieces of property,
much as the furniture, the house and the farmstock
were looked upon. It was the old property right
of man in woman functioning in all its glory, as it
was to continue to function for four thousand years.
The place for a wife, in the full literal significance of
the term, was in her home. Her function in life
was to look after the household, to procreate
children and to rear them. And while the respectable married woman, virtuous to a degree, went
about her menial duties, her lord and husband
flaunted away his leisure hours in the company of
painted women of joy. In all this, it may be argued,
there was nothing that is not customary at the
present day ; which is true enough, except that in
Ancient Greece there was nothing secret or surreptitious in the practices—they were done quite
openly. Both the men's wives and their neighbours
knew all about their carryings on. More, the

highest-class prostitutes, known as *hetairae*, secured respect, attention and honour, without being compelled to have recourse to subterfuge or to disguise their true calling under euphemistic terms. The very fact that they could drive about the streets with their painted faces unveiled proclaimed to all the world exactly what they were, and shouted to the four winds of heaven their forbiddance to take part in certain religious ceremonies, and that any children to which they happened to give birth could never rank as citizens. These *hetairae* were the companions of the wealthiest, most cultured, and most exalted Greeks of the time. They were women of beauty, education, culture and attraction, outshining in every respect the virtuous wives who were engaged in breeding and rearing the children of the race. It was one of these prostitutes, the notorious Aspasia, whose power and influence a queen might well have envied, and whose name has lived through the centuries, who was loved by Alcibiades, Socrates and by scores of others, finally marrying Pericles. Another, by name Bacchis, was the mistress of Hyperides ; yet another, known as Thargelia, was the lover and confidant of Xerxes ; Archaeanassa was the mistress of Plato ; Gnathena lived with Dyphiles ; Phryne had among her numberless lovers Hyperides, Appelles, and Praxiteles. And there were others and again others— the list is endless.

Of course only the most wealthy and influential citizens could afford to consort with these *hetairae*, whose gorgeous upholstery and costly establishments required the bank roll of a millionaire. Demosthenes lavished his fortune on Lais ; on Pythionice the wealth of Babylon was squandered.

The ordinary citizens of Greece had to be content with prostitutes of less charm, and these were looked upon and treated in an altogether different manner from the aristocratic *hetairae*. The temple of Venus at Corinth, which housed a full thousand *dicteriades* or common prostitutes ; and similar temples in Athens and other cities, catered for the sexual wants of the sailors who thronged every port and every town. Here every form of sexual depravity was obtainable at low cost.

The first public brothel of which we have any record was the one which Solon established in Athens.* The inmates were slaves, receiving nothing for their services beyond food and clothing, the fees paid to them going to the State. These whore-houses were known as *dicteria*, and the women who inhabited them as *dicteriades*. Some idea of the number of men who had recourse to the brothels for their sexual requirements is indicated by the fact that out of the profits made through the *dicteria*, a large and ornate temple was built.

Much the same custom seems to have been prevalent throughout the whole of Ancient Greece, though the regulations imposed by Solon were modified, and gradually the prostitute emerged from her one-time slave-like position. But she was compelled to pay taxes to the State. The *dicteriades* remained the lowest class of prostitutes, frequenting the port of Athens, and repairing to the nearest

* Solon justified his action on the ground that prostitution, though an evil, was an essential evil. Incidentally he amassed vast wealth through this project.

dicteria, or to any nearby spot sheltered from the public gaze, with whoever were willing to pay the small fixed price. There appear to have been few restrictions as regards the running of these public brothels. Anyone who could pay the State tax was allowed to open a *dicterion*. So much for the common prostitutes, who were on a par with those found in the lowest type of Continental or South American seaport brothel of the present day.

The female flute-players and dancing girls, known as *auletrides*, were of a much superior class to the common prostitute—superior, that is, in dress, in speech, in bearing. They were engaged at all the banquets, festivals, and suchlike entertainments, public and private ; they were equivalent to the musicians and entertainers which the modern plutocrat hires for his dinner party or private dance. Providing music for the guests was, however, but a small, and a minor part, of the entertainment which these *auletrides* were called upon to furnish. They had to satisfy other appetites. There can be little doubt, judging from references in the works of Athenaeus, Lucian, Antiphanes and contemporary writers, that every form of sexual depravity was pandered to by these girls ; and that these sexual excesses were not confined to men. Tribadism, also, formed a part of their erotic armamentarium. The more talented and beautiful of these flute players were often the lovers of celebrated and powerful men. The famous and notorious Lamia became the mistress of Demelrius, and was deified Venus Lamia after having fabulous wealth lavished upon her and a temple built in her honour.

Turning from Ancient Greece to Rome, we find constant references to prostitution in the works of the oldest historians and litterateurs.* And we find, too, the outlook on prostitution of the inhabitants of Rome, all those thousands of years ago, in close accord with the outlook in England to-day. Unlike the Greeks, the Romans were ashamed to be seen in open companionship with avowed harlots—they skulked and sneaked into the brothels or houses of assignation unknown to their friends and relatives, much in the way in which a respectable man to-day makes overtures to a *fille de joie* in one of the darker and less frequented side streets of the Leicester Square district.

Under Roman law we find the earliest attempts at registration of prostitutes, there being in force a system of inscribing known professional public women similar in its general principles to that now in force in many Continental countries. Indeed, the main difference appears to be that in Rome there was no attempt at medical examination, and it is probable that at that time there was traceable no connection whatever between prostitution and the spread of venereal infection—in fact we have no actual evidence that either syphilis or gonorrhoea were prevalent, or, if prevalent, that they were recognised as diseases of venery.

" Once a prostitute, always a prostitute " was the dictum of the Roman authorities. In other words, if a girl was inscribed as a public prostitute, the giving up of her profession for any reason whatever did not constitute grounds for the removal of her

* See Martial, Plautus, Lacantius and Tacitus.

name from the register. These registered harlots were compelled to wear clothes of a specified uniform type, and to dye their hair yellow or red or blue.*
All these and other regulations were ostensibly designed to discourage girls from taking up the profession, and to degrade in every possible way those who did elect to become prostitutes.**

It is one thing to pass laws dealing with so amorphous and so universal a thing as prostitution ; it is quite another thing to enforce them. And a study of the writings of the Roman historians reveals the fact that there were a very considerable number of prostitutes who practised their profession while managing to evade registration, and in this way, in addition to escaping the branding iron, they evaded payment of the taxes which were collected from their inscribed sisters.

Most of the registered prostitutes practised their profession in brothels, or *lupanaria*, as they were called. They were either inmates permanently or temporarily hired by the owner of the brothel ; or they were street women who rented a room or cell in a brothel when they required the use of it. But by no means all the prostitutes used the brothels. Registered women were not compelled to inhabit *lupanaria*. They could receive their clients in private houses provided they affixed on the doors the nature of their profession and their

* This rule did not apply to the inmates of brothels.

** The real reason behind the wearing of special garments was not *always* with a view to debasing the career of the prostitute, though this may have been paraded to the world. In many cases its sole object was to help the male population to distinguish the women of easy compliance from their more respectable sisters.

fees. The unregistered prostitutes naturally enough could not use the brothels without standing self-confessed as violators of the law, and so they were compelled to use houses where no questions were asked, or to indulge in intercourse in the open, a practice which involved little risk of detection owing to the fact that, in those days, there was no such thing as any form of artificial street-lighting.

In addition to the uninscribed common harlots, there were, as there have been wherever prostitution has flourished, certain females indistinguishable in appearance and in manners from women of respectability, who managed to conceal their true profession from the public. They mixed with the fashionable society of Ancient Rome, they had slaves to attend their wants. These were ostensibly the mistresses of the powerful governors and rulers of the Empire. They were prostitutes of this stamp who ministered to the sensual appetites of Nero, of Vitellius, of Vespasion, of Serverus, of Titus, of Domitian and others. Incest, too, was rife. Domitian had sexual intercourse with his niece ; Nero· committed incest with his own sisters. So, too, did Commodus, whose palace was a brothel populated with three hundred of the most beautiful girls of the age. Elajabalus, pervert and sexual monster, mixed nakedly with the palace harlots day and night.

Mention of prostitution under the ægis of the Romans would be incomplete without some reference to the early Christians, who practised their religion as much as possible in secret. It is a fact common to all countries in which prostitution is officially and publicly frowned upon that the members of the male population view the harlots of foreign or heretical origin with much more complacency than erring females of their own race or religion. The raping of women has always been a part of the persecution meted out to enemy or inferior nations or races both in times of peace and war, and in both savage and civilised countries. According to Suetonius, all virgins who were condemned to death in Ancient Rome, were raped by the executioner before he performed his task. No surprise need be felt then at the practice of compelling Christian virgins, whenever they were discovered, to enter the public brothels. This practice also does something to explain the fact that it was under the ægis of the Christian religion that the beginning of a more charitable and tolerant outlook upon prostitution* manifested itself, and the woman who had sinned in this manner, on repentance, was allowed the benefits and privileges of the Christian religion.

The submission that prostitution was the lesser of two evils, acknowledged by many of the fathers of the Church, was the beginning of a long period of widespread toleration, which gradually extended into approval. The Roman system of regulation and licensing was adopted by one State after another until, in practically every European country, there was some system whereby public women were

---

* It is true that religious prostitution was looked upon not only with tolerance but with approval, but in this connection it is important to remember that at that time these temple harlots were not looked upon or known as prostitutes at all—they were " priestesses " or " wives " of the deity.

available in certain quarters of the big cities. In many cases the State or the city benefited by the taxes which the prostitutes, or the owners of the brothels, were called upon to contribute.

In the Middle Ages, so important a part in the life of the city did the brothels become, that it was customary for the city authorities to cause the more important brothels to place their inmates at the disposal of royalty, celebrities or other important guests of the city, without any charge. In Burchard's *Diary* occurs a description of an orgy in the private rooms of the Pope, where, after supper, fifty naked prostitutes danced for the amusement of the Pope's guests, among whom were the notorious Caesar and Lucrezia Borgia. At this time a considerable portion of the Pope's income consisted of a tax on brothels. This attitude, whereby the State or the city derived from the brothels considerable financial benefit, and important personages secured amusement in addition, was common throughout Europe. In 1347 Queen Johanna of Naples arranged for a city brothel at Avignon, to which free access was given to all men of rank or celebrity. On the occasion of the visit of the Emperor Sigismund to Ulm in 1434, the royal suite visited the common brothels. Every royal palace had its own brothel, and every royal tour had its accompanying band of prostitutes, too. Charles the Bold maintained a retinue of at least four thousand for the use of himself and his court. Every moving army similarly was followed by hordes of harlots. The Crusaders had thousands at their heels ; each camp maintaining its own large brothel. Even the devout Francis I had a collection of " camp-followers " who were paid for their services, as is shown in the royal account books. In more recent times, these " camp followers," though none the less existent, have been dignified by more euphemistic names. Thus, during the world war, there are ample reasons for assuming that a considerable number of the women who, in various guises and under a miscellany of names, were attached to the armies, really served the troops in a capacity which is usually expected from professional street women.

In these days, owing to the hypocritical attitude adopted by many governments, and especially by all English-speaking peoples, towards prostitution, such a state of affairs as prevailed in the Middle Ages appears extraordinarily vulgar and immoral. But to understand the position it must be remembered that at that time intercourse with a common prostitute, or openly visiting a brothel, was looked upon with no more reprobation than in these days one looks upon a visit to a night club or a carousal in a public house. So ordinary and so necessary an amusement was a visit to a brothel conceded to be that it was the custom for important public dignatories and officials, when travelling on business connected with the State, to charge, as part of their legitimate travelling expenses, the cost of visiting public brothels in the towns where they stayed the night. Some shadow of this attitude towards prostitution still persists in certain Continental and foreign States, where patronage of brothels and sleeping with harlots are both looked upon as mild peccadillos and openly admitted. Probably, however, at no period in history have prostitutes—whose profession was openly admitted and brazenly described by its real name—ranked higher than they did in the fourteenth and fifteenth centuries. The brothels attached to the royal palaces were sumptuous apartments ; the women who were chosen to grace them were, so long as they remained in favour, elegantly attired. The official who was in charge of the royal brothel, and whose duties were those of a modern pimp or procurer, far from being shunned and looked down upon as a contemptible and criminal debauchee, held considerable rank and was known as " King of the Prostitutes." His female assistant—the counterpart of the modern brothel *madame*—was similarly a court official in whom was vested much authority and dignity.

With the coming of the Reformation, the policy of concealing the real profession of these women under a variety of fancy and euphemistic names flourished once again in all its old glory. This policy was extended and developed all through the ages, reaching its higher and more decorative forms in the *demi-mondaines* and *grandes cocottes* of Italy and France ; the " demi-reps " of England ; and their prototypes in civilised countries the world over.

In the old days even, many of the brothels were dignified by politer names. Often they were called baths. In point of fact every existent public bath in the Middle Ages was a brothel. The connection between bathing and venery, which is well known to every sexologist, was also not unknown to the

ancients. As long ago as the time of Mohammed
we find that old sage and law-giver saying : " All
the earth is given to me as a place of prayer, and
as pure, except the burial ground and the bath."
The notorious ' stews ' (baths) of London were
neither more nor less than common whore-houses.*
They were mostly found in the Borough of Southwark, near the palace of the Bishop of Winchester,
who at that time obtained a big income from the
rents of these ' stews.' Certain regulations were
imposed by Parliament respecting the conditions to
be observed by those renting the brothels, and by
those using them. A prostitute was compelled to
lie with her mate the whole night—in no case was
one of the brothels to be used as what, in modern
terminology, is called " a short-time house." Nor
was a prostitute, or the keeper of the " stew-
house," allowed to entice men to enter. No
woman suffering from a venereal disease (" burning ")** was allowed to be an inmate ; nor was a
woman known to be married. The " stews " were
searched once a week by a constable or other officer
of the law. In 1545, the eighth Henry. urged on
by the Reformation party, closed the " stews " of
Southwark, and thus ended England's first and only
experiment in the provision of brothels for the
purposes of prostitution.

The end of this long period of toleration and

* The close connection between baths and promiscuity or perversion
appears to have been universally recognised throughout the civilised
world of that date. More recently, in 1649, the scheme of one, Peter
Chamberlin, to build baths in all English cities, failed, upon the ground
of morality, to receive the sanction of Parliament.

** This would appear to have been the first attempt to prevent the spread
of venereal infection, not only in England but in any country.

approval, and of a degree of licentiousness without parallel in modern history, came at last, and with it a strong reaction of feeling against prostitution and prostitutes, resulting in wholesale attempts at suppression and punishment. From the beginning of history there have been fortuitous attempts, usually on the part of some individual ruler, to suppress or regulate prostitution, but nothing in any way like the campaign which swept the larger part of Europe in the sixteenth century. These attempts, and this changed attitude, are usually regarded as due to a re-awakening of morality and religion in the people, and especially in the men at the heads of the various countries. The assumption is an erroneous one. It was due to neither religion nor morality. It was due to fear of disease. At this time syphilis had obtained a firm hold in several European countries, and there can be little doubt that the charge brought against the prostitutes and the public brothels, of extending the prevalence of the disease, though considerably exaggerated, had a good deal of truth in it. The rich, the powerful, and the celebrated alike ceased to patronise the brothels, and, once these personages were no longer personally interested in the dens of vice as sources of amusement and of revenue, they were willing to don the reformer's cloak and give heed to the outcry against prostitution and the women connected with it. State and Church united in a harrying of these unfortunate women which at times reached unparalleled levels of cruelty.

CHAPTER X

ATTEMPTS AT SUPPRESSION

Since the first appearance of professional prostitution fugitive efforts have been made to stamp it out of existence. There have always been moralists and others who, for one reason or another, have disagreed with the apologetic argument that prostitution is a necessary evil, and, in the main, these members of the opposing party have been responsible for the attempts at suppression.

Punishment by whipping and by various forms of torture was often the means chosen ; occasionally prostitutes were driven from the towns and cities and sometimes out of the country ; more rarely mayhem and the death penalty were imposed.

The most ancient efforts at suppression of which we have any record appear to be the closing of the Roman brothels by Valentinian and the younger Theodosius. Justinian adopted similar measures, and threw all concerned with prostitution into exile, while treating the harlots themselves with considerable leniency and devising means to assist their reformation, as, for instance, in removing all barriers to their marriage and entry into respectability. The Empress Theodora, who was a prostitute herself when Justinian married her, encouraged these reformative measures and built a retreat of some magnificence for the housing of penitent harlots.

The efforts at suppression merely served to drive the trade into the adoption of hole and corner methods, and we find in every period of oppression and persecution that prostitution still existed in surreptitious forms, breaking out into the open the moment a more tolerant attitude prevailed.

The toleration of the early Christians caused great extension in both brothel and clandestine prostitution. Then, in the sixth century, Recared, a king of the Visogoths, ordered every prostitute to be punished with three hundred strokes of the whip before being driven out of the city. After this, apart from a few half-hearted attempts at suppression, prostitution flourished gaily in profligate Europe for a matter of five hundred years at the most modest of estimates. There were brothels everywhere, flourishing as baths and under other euphemised names. The nunneries and the monasteries were either brothels or places where perverse sexual acts were openly practised.

Indeed for centuries nearly every European city was overrun with prostitutes. It must be remembered that licentiousness was the rule rather than the exception. Paris swarmed with harlots of every class. So did Rome. So did London. So did Venice. In Strasburgh there were whores openly soliciting in every place of worship.

So we arrive at the reign of Louis IX. of France, the first French king to make any really sincere effort to put an end to a state of affairs which was making Paris notorious throughout all the marches of Europe. In 1254, Louis made an edict which imposed exile from France upon every prostitute, every brothel-keeper and every procurer. But the cure, as is so often the case, was found to be a good deal worse than the disease. Women of respectability were, by one means or another, induced to satisfy the appetites of those who had been in the habit of frequenting the brothels. Saint Augustine's old dictum proved true—the virtue of respectable womanhood was safe only so long as professional prostitution existed to satisfy the sexual cravings of mankind. After an experiment extending over a couple of years, Louis removed his edict, and the prostitutes flocked back to the re-opened brothels. They were, however, compelled to observe certain rules. They were restricted to certain parts of Paris ; they were not allowed to wear meretricious apparel ; they were supervised by an official. In short, Louis made an attempt at regulation something after the Roman style, but it proved of small value, and finally it was abolished. Philip, successor to Louis, made fitful attempts to suppress prostitution, but actually they proved of little or no avail.

All these and similar efforts continued to be put into force spasmodically and from time to time. But, as I have already indicated, there was no really serious effort made until the rapid expansion of the incidence of syphilis, and the blame for its spreading falling upon the harlots, caused general alarm throughout Europe.

The sailors who took part in the expedition of Columbus to the New World are supposed to be responsible for introducing syphilis into Europe on their return to Spain in 1494. While the contention that before this time syphilis was unknown in Europe is extremely dubious, it is certain that in the early fifteen hundreds syphilis and gonorrhoea (the two venereal infections were thought, at that time, to be manifestations of one disease) reached a peak of universality hitherto unknown, spreading rapidly throughout every part of the Continent. While the sailors of Columbus were accused of bringing the infection to Spain, the occupants of the brothels were blamed for spreading it wholesale among the male members of the community. Soon after the commencement of the sixteenth century we find brothels and their inmates being attacked in all the countries of Europe.

Thus in France, in 1560, Charles IX. was responsible for an edict which abolished Parisian brothels, compelling all prostitutes and those connected with the profession to leave the city. In Italy, in 1577, every prostitute and every brothel-keeper were given eight days in which to remove themselves from Catalina, the penalty being whipping for the prostitute and the galleys for the brothel-keepers. In Spain, although prostitutes were allowed in the cities, they were compelled to submit to examination by a physician, and if found to be infected were not allowed to practice their profession.

Naturally, these attempts failed to abolish or even to curtail seriously the incidence or extent of prostitution. They merely sufficed to make both the prostitutes and their clients much more careful, and where brothels were actually abolished, secret prostitution took the place of open prostitution.

Then, too, the waves of persecution, when, and as they arose, brought in their train many evils. The laws against prostitution were made to serve other purposes, and men got rid of their mistresses and concubines by accusing them of being professional harlots and having them banished from the district.

It would serve no useful purpose, and it would prove dreary reading, to trace in detail the many attempts at suppression which were attempted through the centuries. Each period of rigorous persecution was followed, in most cases, by a more tolerant attitude, and thus the history of prostitution in Europe is marked by apparent bursts of the most flagrant licentiousness interposed between more moral times. Whipping and other more cruel forms of punishment, exile, imprisonment were all tried again and again, and just as often they all failed. By the time of the Napoleonic wars it was generally recognised throughout Continental Europe that all attempts to suppress the trade were futile.

In America, however, and in England, the moral and religious elements had not given up the fight for suppression. As recently as 1891 an attempt was made to clear out the prostitutes in Pittsburg and in New York City. The brothels and assignment houses were closed, the prostitutes were turned into the streets and tradespeople and landladies were requested to refuse to provide them with either food or lodgings. These measures were drastic and they were cruel, but they failed to produce any permanent good effects—all they did was to drive the women to other towns for the time being.

In England, during the nineteenth century, an attempt at suppression was made at Portsmouth. An account of this effort was given by a witness before the Select Committee appointed in 1879 to inquire into the operation and effects of the Contagious Diseases Acts, and from this account, as given by Havelock Ellis,* it appears that the mayor of that city, in 1860, was evidently imbued with the idea of stamping out the prostitution which, at that time, was rampant. To this end, between three hundred and four hundred prostitutes were driven out of their lodgings into the streets. The workhouse, to which they went for succour, refused to admit them, and so, homeless and hungry, they marched the streets for days on end. No one wanted them. There was no place for them to go. In the end the authorities allowed them to return to their lodgings and to pursue their career. The experiment in suppression was a complete failure.

These American and English experiments seem to have been the last efforts at actual suppression. Their failure marked a universal agreement among the bitterest opponents of prostitution on a policy of despair.

* Havelock Ellis, *Studies in the Psychology of Sex*, Vol. VI, Davis, Philadelphia, 1927, p. 248.

CHAPTER XI

THE REGULATION OF PROSTITUTION

As it became obvious that not only was it quite impossible to suppress prostitution, but that in nearly every instance any attempt at suppression brought in its train evils which were at least as bad as the disease itself, the thoughts of reformers and moralists gradually turned from suppression to regulation. It was contended that an evil which could not be eradicated was best controlled.

We have seen that the regulation of prostitution and the licensing of brothels extend as far back as the time of Solon, and that in various cities of Europe certain regulations were imposed upon brothels and their inmates. But all such attempts at regulation, arising out of religious prostitution, were mainly concerned with raising money for the Church or the State. Eighteenth century regulation was concerned primarily with the health and the morals of the community, and only secondarily and incidentally with taxation.

It is true that after the spread of syphilis in Europe, some feeble, fitful, half-hearted attempts had been made in the way of medically examining prostitutes, but these measures were not adopted to any serious extent or with any degree of thoroughness. It was not until the eighteenth century that anything in this line worthy of consideration was attempted. Various authorities and various countries have been credited with inaugurating the system of medical examination which was eventually to spread throughout most of Continental Europe, but the truth of the matter seems to be that most countries awoke to the need for some such system about the same time. Thus in Berlin, an enactment of 1700, dealing with prostitution, made provision for all professional harlots to be examined by a surgeon once a fortnight. In 1724, Bernard Mandeville, an English writer, in his notorious pamphlet, *A Modest Defense of Publick Stews*, advocated the medical inspection of prostitutes frequenting brothels, but his arguments were received without approval. All this time prostitution was increasing ; and all this time, too, venereal disease was spreading by leaps and bounds. By the end of the century, through the incidence of the French Revolution and the series of wars it brought in its train, syphilis and gonorrhoea were rampant, and prostitutes flaunted their charms brazenly in every big city of Europe.

The first attempt at registration in France was the system introduced in 1778, but it was Napoleon, at the height of his fame and power, who was responsible for the establishment in Paris of the first really adequate system of medical examination of prostitutes. Actually, the system was first introduced in 1802, but it was not until some twenty years later that it was perfected and became in general use throughout the Parisian brothels. This French system, it is worthy of mention, is not based upon a law applying universally to all towns, cities, *et al.* Each municipal authority is empowered to take such steps as are deemed advisable in the interests of public order and health. It is for this reason that regulation is not in force in every French city.*

In England many attempts have been made to institute a system of regulation. The earliest of these attempts of which there is any record was the sanctioning by Parliament in 1161 of the establishment of brothels (" stews ") in the city of London, where they were permitted to flourish for nearly four hundred years. Public opinion in Great Britain has always been against the regulation or the licensing of prostitutes, largely because it is felt that any such regulation amounts to a justification of the evil. This attitude on the part of the English people and the English government has been considered, by foreigners, to be a hypocritical attitude. And, admittedly, so it is. But hypocritical or not, the English people may be considered to be definitely opposed to any system of licensing and medical inspection. For the licensing system *has* been tried in England. The experiment, now long forgotten, is of such importance in any study of prostitution that it is worthy of consideration in some detail.

The reason for the putting into operation of this system of licensing was through the fact that a committee was appointed by the Admiralty in 1862 to consider the question of venereal disease in the

---

* The brothel system has now been abandoned in Strassbourg, Sedan, Nancy, Grenoble, and several other towns.

Army and Navy, and the regulation of prostitution. This Committee's findings were against the compulsory medical examination of prostitutes, but they considered that it would be advisable to take steps to induce these women to submit voluntarily to examination and, if diseased, to enter special hospitals for treatment. However, these details were not presented to the public ; but when, on June 20, 1864, Lord Clarence Paget, Secretary to the Admiralty, presented the Bill which was later to be the subject of such widespread public indignation and bitter controversy, in the debate in the House of Commons the grave state of health in the Army and Navy generally through the ravages of venereal infections was the justification given for the measures embodied in the proposed Act. The Bill, known as the Contagious Diseases Prevention Act, 1864, was finally placed upon the statute book in July of that year.

Briefly stated, the Act provided for the compulsory examination of any woman believed to be " a common prostitute," and if found to be suffering from a venereal disease, for her detention in a Lock hospital for a period not exceeding three months. The Act applied to the garrison towns of Portsmouth, Plymouth, Woolwich, Chatham, Sheerness, Aldershot, Colchester, Shorncliffe, the Curragh, Cork and Queenstown—the idea of its promoters was to give it a three years' trial. Two years later a further Act was passed to take effect on the expiration of the 1864 Act. This new Act extended the features of the existent one, by providing for the registration of prostitutes and their compulsory regular medical examination, thus embodying the main features of the registration system in vogue in so many Continental states. It also added Windsor to the list of towns. Then, in 1869, another Act added Canterbury, Dover, Gravesend, Maidstone, Winchester and Southampton to the list.

The Acts were not operated by the ordinary police. A special body of plain-clothes officers was embodied in each of the towns in which the Acts applied. Virtually these officials were private detectives, and their duties consisted in discovering any women who were engaged in professional promiscuity. Every woman who was found to be a prostitute had her name and address entered upon a special register, and once a name was entered it could not be removed without permission. The object of this register was to place in the hands of the police a means whereby known prostitutes could be compelled to present themselves at regular intervals for medical examination. Thus once a fortnight each woman whose name appeared on the register must submit to medical inspection or become liable to arrest and imprisonment. So long as the registered woman remained healthy she was allowed to ply her trade ; if, on examination, she proved to be infected with syphilis, gonorrhoea, or soft chancre (the three contagious venereal infections), she was packed off to a hospital where she was to all intents and purposes a prisoner. And there she was detained until supposedly cured of the infection.

It is obvious that the scheme, whichever way one looks at it, was a bad one. Its aim was not to prevent prostitution, but to support it ; not to discourage fornication, but to enable members of the forces to indulge in promiscuity with safety. Its marked punitive feature was the imprisonment— for the hosptials were really prisons masquerading under a euphemistic name—of the woman for suffering from a disease which she might have, and probably had, acquired from the party for whose benefit the scheme was supposedly and ostensibly inaugurated.

The special body of police in plain clothes who administered the law, made every effort to " find " women who made a profession of prostitution, and, when found, to force them to sign what was termed a " voluntary submission." The signing of this form by any woman amounted to an admission that she was a prostitute, and an undertaking to present herself for fortnightly medical examination. Once signed there was no such thing as retraction— even the giving up of prostitution in favour of regular respectable employment or of marriage was not in itself sufficient to render her free from the necessity of presenting herself for examination. To secure such exemption a magistrate's order was required, and there were many difficulties in the way of obtaining such an order. If the woman refused to sign the " voluntary submission " form, the officer applied to a magistrate for a summons on the ground that he had " good cause to believe " her to be " a common prostitute," and invariably the result was that the woman was compelled to submit in the end to registration.

There can be no question whatever but that the Acts led to wholesale injustice, as anyone with experience of the workings of officialdom in any part of the world can very well imagine. The police bullied the girls and women into signing the form, and, as they never explained the nature of its contents, and as, further, in those days, the bulk of women of the servant and peasant class were unable to read, in very many instances they had not the slightest conception of what they were signing. In this connection Benjamin Scott, who has written a detailed and documented history of the long struggle which culminated in the repeal of one of the most notoriously unjust and tyrannical pieces of legislation that has ever blackened the English statute book, says :

" Mr. Ryder, a Justice of the Peace for Devonport, and friendly to the system, said to the Royal Commission in 1871, ' I believe that almost every woman who has been brought before the Justices has complained that she has signed the submission *without being aware of what she was doing!* The House Surgeon at the Royal Albert Hospital, Devonport, said, ' The women have often told me that they *did not know what they were signing.* . . . I think the greater number of these women who signed the *voluntary* submission were induced to do so by pressure, and that many of them were ignorant of the character of the document which they signed. *Mere children* were induced to sign it '."*

* Benjamin Scott, *A State Iniquity : Its Rise, Extension and Overthrow,* Kegan Paul, 1890, p. 24.

Certainly many women, and especially young girls who were not prostitutes at all, were placed on the register, and the fear of these disguised police and the powers they wielded, made life for decent women in the towns covered by the Acts a matter of some anxiety. In his official report for the year 1873, Colonel Henderson, the Chief of the Metropolitan Police, said : " The presence of the officers employed is well known to the class of girls most likely to go astray, and the dread of detection is very salutary. In proof of this, young women in the position of domestic servants and others, after nightfall, leave their male acquaintances directly the police employed under the Acts appear in sight." A more blatant and shameful admission of official bullying and intimidation from the lips of a responsible public servant cannot well be imagined. Actually the women in the garrison towns were terrorized by the police officials and by others who impersonated them for the purpose of levying blackmail.

Naturally enough the Acts and the manner of carrying out their provisions, came in for a considerable amount of criticism, and gradually there sprang up in the country a good deal of hostile feeling, especially as those responsible for and in favour of these Acts and their administration were anxious to extend their zone of application so as to embrace towns in all parts of the kingdom. As a result of this controversy and the continually growing distaste for the official bullying and interference, two associations were formed with the specific common object of securing the repeal of the Acts. Many prominent men and women worked tooth and nail to this end, foremost among whom were Daniel Cooper, James Stansfield, Florence Nightingale, Harriett Martineau, and Josephine Butler. Even so, progress was slow and wearisomely difficult, and it was not until 1886 that the Acts were actually repealed.*

Although there have always been, and there are today, plenty of English legislators and reformers in favour of the regulation of prostitution, since that day no serious attempt has been made to reintroduce any system of registration and medical examination of prostitutes. For the ill-starred wartime measure of 1918 can hardly be dignified by inclusion in the category of systems for the regulation of prostitution.**

Turning to the United States of America, it appears that an initial attempt at regulation was made about the same time as the English experiment. A colonel of the United States Army, one Fletcher, attached to the Surgeon-General's Office, and who claimed to be the first to attempt any " systematic inspection of prostitutes " in the United States, along with another medical officer,

---

* An Act on similar lines to the Contagious Diseases Act, compelling common prostitutes to submit to medical examination, was in force in Queensland, Australia, from 1868 to 1911. In 1911 it was repealed by the Health Acts Amendment Act, which makes it compulsory for prostitutes to be medically examined.

** Owing to venereal disease in the army reaching such enormous proportions, a regulation (40d), dealing with diseased prostitutes, was added to the Defence of the Realm Act. It empowered the authorities to force any woman to submit herself to medical examination if accused by a member of H.M. Forces of having infected him with a venereal disease. It presented, obviously, opportunities for vindictive allegations and gross injustice. It was repealed within a year of adoption.

at Nashville, in 1863, instituted a system whereby public women were compelled to present themselves for medical examination at ten-day intervals. In the appendix to Sanger's book there is an account of this experiment,* given in Fletcher's own words, and as presented by him to the Committee appointed in 1879 to consider the question of venereal diseases and their prevention. According to this account, the system was in operation three years, and Colonel Fletcher claimed that it led to a marked decrease in the incidence of venereal disease. It does not seem to be clear, however, why, in view of this, the Nashville experiment was not continued or similar schemes attempted elsewhere.

The next attempt at regulation, on the lines advocated by Sanger himself, who was strongly in favour of the licensing of prostitutes and their systematic medical inspection, was made in 1872, in the middle-western city of St. Louis. All women engaged in the profession of prostitution, whether they were brothel inmates, street-walkers, or mistresses, were compelled to be registered and to submit to weekly inspection. If once a woman was entered on the register she must notify the police on making any change of address, whether within the city of St. Louis or elsewhere. The statute was, however, short-lived, lasting barely a year. So strong was the opposition to what was described by its opponents as " the licensing of vice " that, after the presentation of a petition bearing over a

* William W. Sanger, *The History of Prostitution*. Medical Publishing Co., New York, 1919.

hundred thousand signatures, the authorities were compelled to remove the statute.

Since that day no serious attempt has been made to reintroduce the registration of prostitutes, but the famous Page law of 1910 contains a clause (Section 79) providing for the medical examination of any prostitute convicted as a vagrant. This clause is of such importance that I think it well to reproduce it in full :

" *Section 79. Medical Examination of Prostitutes.*"

" On and after the first day of September, nineteen hundred and ten, any person who is a vagrant, as defined in subdivision four of section eight hundred and eighty-seven of the code of criminal procedure, or who is convicted of a violation of subdivision two of section fourteen hundred and fifty-eight of the consolidation act, or of section one hundred and fifty of the tenement-house law, shall after conviction be taken to a room adjacent to the court room, and there be physically examined by a woman physician of the department of health detailed for such purpose. After such examination the physician making the same shall promptly prepare and sign a written report to the Court of the prisoner's physical condition, and if it thereby appears that the prisoner is afflicted with any venereal disease which is contagious, infectious, or communicable, the magistrate shall commit her to a public hospital having a ward or wards for the treatment of the disease with which she is afflicted, for detention and treatment for a minimum period fixed by him in the commitment and for a maximum period of not more than one year : provided, that in case a prisoner so committed to any institution shall be cured of her venereal disease, which is contagious, infectious, or communicable, after the expiration of the minimum period and before the expiration of the maximum period for which she was committed to such institution, she shall be discharged and released from custody upon the written order of the officer in charge of the institution to which she was committed, upon the certificate of a physician of such institution or of the department of health that the prisoner is free of any venereal disease which is contagious, infectious, or communicable. If, however, such prisoner shall be cured, prior to the expiration of the minimum period for which she was committed, she shall be forthwith transferred to the workhouse and discharged at the expiration of said minimum period. Nothing herein contained shall be construed to limit the authority of a city magistrate to commit any prisoner for an indeterminate period to any institution now having authority by law to receive inmates for detention for a period of more than one year."

It will be seen that this regulation applies only to such prostitutes as have been convicted under the Vagrancy Act. But even so, it allows openings for much unfairness, and has been the subject of a considerable amount of hostile criticism. We shall consider this point in some detail, however, in a subsequent chapter.

To-day, there are few American or Canadian cities with " red-light " districts, these having been abolished in deference to public opinion. Before the war, practically every city of any size in the United States had its " red-light " district. The abolition of brothels and houses of assignation blatantly proclaiming their trade, does not, however, imply their non-existence, any more than it does in English cities. They flourish in innumerable surreptitious forms, and they secure their clientele through " underground " channels or by means of carefully-worded advertisements.

CHAPTER XII

CONCUBINES AND " KEPT WOMEN "

ALTHOUGH, strictly speaking, according to definition and according to law, neither a concubine nor
a mistress is a prostitute, in real life the line
between the one and the other is so difficult to
designate and so very often overlaps, that in any
study of prostitution some attention must be given
to both these social types. And it may safely be
asserted that just as in the past nearly every
concubine was guilty of prostitution either incidentally or fortuitously, so to-day there are few "kept
women " who do not ply the prostitute's profession
in some form or other and under the protective
covering which their lover's patronage provides.

A concubine is an unmarried woman who lives
in the same house as a man, has sexual intercourse
with him, and is supported by him. She is not kept
in an apartment and visited by him at intervals, as
so often happens in the case of the modern " kept
woman " or mistress, but she shares the same
household as the man who supports her. Actually,
however, the term " kept woman " has displaced,
in modern civilisation, the term " concubine," which
may now be looked upon as obsolete.

In ancient times concubines were plentiful ;
nearly every wealthy and powerful man having one

or more, and neither the fact of keeping a concubine in one's household nor of being a concubine, was looked upon as a disgrace. And while it was strictly forbidden, in the Mosaic code, for a father to allow his daughter to become a prostitute, thus : " Do not prostitute thy daughter, to cause her to be a whore ; lest the land fall to whoredom, and the land become full of wickedness " (Leviticus xix. 29), the right of the father to sell his daughter into concubinage was admitted.* Even Moses himself had a concubine.

In certain cases where the legally wedded wife proved impotent, the husband took to himself another woman for the purpose of begetting children.** This practice was common in Germany at one time.

According to Thomasius,*** concubinage was prevalent in all countries and for many generations. It was permitted by both Church and State. Evidently the legal wife did not resent the presence in her house of a concubine—the fact that she occupied the superior position probably accounting for her tolerant attitude.

These women were attached to both married and single men. Almost every priest had his concubine, though she was usually known by another and more euphemistic name. Saint

* According to Dufour (*Historie de la Prostitution*) a concubine was under the same sexual obligation to the man responsible for her keep, as was his wife—both could be accused of committing adultery.

** In those days the blame for the failure to beget children was invariably placed upon the woman ; the possibility of the man being sterile never occurred to anyone.

*** Thomasius, *De Concubinata*.

Augustine did much towards moulding the tolerant attitude of the Christian Church towards concubinage, which is not very much to be wondered at seeing that before he had his religious visions he possessed a concubine himself.

With the coming of the Reformation a gradual change took place in the attitude of the Church toward concubinage. No longer were the authorities able to wink at the practice of priests openly living with women of easy virtue.

The history of prostitution, and of sexual morals, is largely an account of putting fresh labels on old bottles. There has never, from the beginning of time, been any decline in the appetite of man for sexual intercourse with woman. To the contrary, there has been a development of that appetite under civilisation, more comfortable environmental conditions, and higher standards of living. There has never been any decline in man's appetite for sexual adventure with strange women ; or with as many different women as his means permitted or opportunity presented. Thus, any interference with or prohibition by the State or by the Church of a special form of sexual adventure was followed by the creation of another analogous form or the practice of the same form under different terminology or in other circumstances. The prohibition of concubinage by the Church had not the slightest effect in limiting or preventing either priests or ordinary mortals indulging in sexual intercourse outside the marital state. It merely resulted in the priest turning out of his home the concubine that had graced it, and visiting her surreptitiously in a house or an apartment which he provided for her. All through the ages, religion has proved itself well able to provide means for the indulgence in sexual intercourse by its leaders, while ostensibly frowning upon and vigorously denouncing any manifestations of the sexual urge among its more humble members.

As we have seen, the pagans of old, working upon the credulity, ignorance and superstition of the people, justified the right of the priest, acting in the capacity of God's surrogate, to rape virgin girls. They devised means for forcing the women to act as prostitutes in the service of God. With the coming of Christianity they succeeded in inducing attractive women to become " consecrated " servants of God ; in other words, concubines of the priests. With the passing of the concubine, the nuns in the convents provided the " holy men " with the means of satisfying their sexual cravings. In many cases special religions arose, with which were associated sexual practices and orgies of the most licentious and, occasionally, the most repulsive nature. Thus, the early Christian sexual orgies connected with the Shrove Tuesday festivals ; the coprophagy of Ezekiel ; the flagellation of the Konigsberg pietists ; the obscene rites associated with the devil worship of the Middle Ages. And, coming to comparatively modern days, the Oneida Community practised a perverse form of coitus under the name of morality and religion ; the Mormons, for generations, indulged in polygamy with impunity ; the notorious " Abode of Love " was little better than a brothel. Even to-day it is possible, in the name of religion, to carry out practices which would, in any other circumstances, earn the most severe censure and probably lead to a criminal prosecution.

While the " men of God " have distinct advantages in this connection, others possessed of wealth and influence have always found it an easy matter to indulge in their sexual appetites while continuing outwardly to wear the cloak of respectability. The passing of the concubine in European countries led to the establishment of " kept women " in apartments. In this way married men successfully prevented their mistresses and their wives coming in contact. Even if concubinage had not come in for religious and moral denunciation, it is more than probable that the " kept woman " housed in special apartments, usually well away from the man's ordinary residence, would have found favour both with kings and with commoners.

It was by no means unusual for the mistress of a king or an emperor to wield the power of a queen. There have been innumerable instances in English and Continental history of royal mistresses possessing such influence. Among the most famous in English records are Rosamond, the mistress of Henry II. ; Jane Shore, who lived with Edward IV. and Nell Gwyn, Charles's notorious paramour.

The beautiful Rosamond, called the Fair, who, strangely enough, was sanctified by the populace after her death, was the mother of Henry's two sons, the Earl of Salisbury and the Bishop of London. Jane Shore, favourite of Edward IV., and the wife of a London goldsmith, afterwards became the mistress of Lord Hastings ; Nell Gwyn, reared

I

in a brothel, first an orange girl and then an actress,* after being the mistress of Lord Buckhurst, became Charles's favourite, and was known by the name she gave herself—" the Protestant whore."

Not in all the annals of English history, however, is there for the finding any instance where a king's mistress wielded such power or squandered such an amount of money as did the famous Madame du Barry, for five years mistress of the profligate French King, Louis XV. For five years this woman, of dubious parentage, illiterate, ex-slut of the streets, ruled over Louis' fashionable court with a power that no woman other than Catherine of Russia and Elizabeth of England ever rivalled. In those five years she drained the coffers of the French Treasury to a degree that is staggering in its immensity ; she is estimated to have spent the colossal sum of twelve million pounds. Only the death of Louis put an end to this monstrous profligacy in the expenditure of public money.

But French history bristles with instances where royal mistresses of obscure origin have wielded great influence and squandered money right and left. Madame de Maintenon was one such. She was a widow and a governess ; she was not much of a beauty, she had not even youth to bless herself with, but she became the mistress of Louis XIV. Not one of his former favourites—and they were many—with all their youth and beauty, ever had a

---

* In the days of Charles II. most actresses were prostitutes. The orange girls, so-called because they peddled oranges inside the theatres, were really prostitutes of the lowest type, who made lewd jokes with, and told obscene stories to the men who patronised the theatres.

tithe of the power which this older woman wielded over the king and his country. For thirty-five years —no less—she virtually ruled France.

Another notorious mistress, but of a different brand, was Gabrielle d'Estrées, afterwards Duchesse of Beaufort, one of the fifty women with whom Henri IV., first as King of Navarre and then as King of France, had associations. She supplanted the lovely Marguerite de Valois, who after being divorced by her fat, gluttonous, dirty and dissipated husband, embarked upon a career of libidinage almost unparalleled in history.

Somewhat allied to the mistress was the courtesan,* who made her appearance in Continental Europe during the Middle Ages. The courtesan was really a high-class prostitute moving in aristocratic circles, and in many respects resembling the *hetairae* of Ancient Greece. She differed from the mistress in that she was not kept by, or connected with, one man only. Usually she controlled her own establishment, and chose her lovers with care and discretion. The salons of many of the more celebrated courtesans were the meeting places for celebrities in the literary, artistic and social worlds. Usually the courtesan, like the *hetairae* of Greece, was a woman whose education, intelligence and accomplishments exceeded by far those of the average woman of her day and even most of the ladies of the aristocracy. It was for this reason, in addition to her mastery of the art of love, that she

---

* Originally ' Courtesan ' was a term used to describe a lady who was attached to the court. Today the word is used as a synonym for prositute and is applied to all but the lowest types of brothel harlots and ' sailors' women.'

was sought after by the most influential men of her time. Veronico Franco, the Italian courtesan, was poet as well as prostitute, the confidant and intimate of Tintoret, Henri III. of France, and a host of others. Tullia d'Aragona was just such another. Marion de Lorme, described by the Count de Grammont as " the most charming creature in all France," had the aristocracy of the day at her feet.

Perhaps, however, the most famous of them all was Ninon de l'Enclos—the immortal Ninon. Many writers have affirmed, possibly in their whitewashing zeal, that the beautiful Ninon was not, in actual fact, a prostitute at all, basing their assertions on the fact that she refused to accept money from her miscellany of lovers. But valuable presents are often equivalent to money, and of these she was offered and she accepted enough to make any modern *fille de joie's* mouth water in sheer envy. Her magnificent salon in Paris attracted the best brains of Europe. Her opinions and her criticisms were valued by men of the highest mentality. Moliere let her read his famous *Tartuffe* in manuscript ; Scarron and Saint-Evremond sought her opinion on their works before publication. Coligny, the Marquis de Villarceaux, Huyghens, the Comte de Tallard, the Marquis de Sévigné, the Duc de la Rochefoucauld, all in turn were her lovers.

PART III

PROSTITUTION TO-DAY

CHAPTER XIII

MODERN PRACTITIONERS OF THE OLDEST PROFESSION— BROTHEL AND CLANDESTINE PROSTITUTES

PROFESSIONAL prostitution to-day flourishes in many forms, the precise form or forms flourishing in different countries, and in different parts of the same country, varying considerably. For instance, there are no brothel prostitutes in England, as there are in so many Continental and foreign countries. On the other hand, street-walkers, which are so common in English cities, are rarely seen in many foreign countries. Then again, in some States, prostitutes are registered, in others there is no system of regulation whatever. Usually, brothels and registration go together, though there are registered prostitutes who are not inmates of brothels or in any way connected with them. It would appear to be customary in all regulationist countries (i.e., countries where there is a system of registration and medical inspection) to regard prostitution as an evil which must be endured ; and in all non-regulationist or abolitionist countries (i.e., countries where there is no registration or medical inspection) to ignore the question of prostitution except where and so far as it can be linked with some other offence and penalized or punished vicariously. The modern tendency is undoubtedly against regulation, as is instanced by the steady decline in the number of countries adopting registration. At the time of writing, the following States have neither licensed houses nor registration of prostitutes : Alsace, Czechoslovakia, Denmark, Finland, Germany, Great Britain, Iceland, Ireland (including Irish Free State), Netherlands, Norway, Russia, Sweden, Switzerland, Palestine, Burma, Australia (except Queensland),* Canada, New Zealand, South Africa, United States of America, Brazil, Bolivia, Dominican Republic. In certain countries brothels have been abolished, though some form of registration is in force, thus Bulgaria, Estonia, Hungary, Latvia, Lithuania, Luxemburg, Monaco, Poland, Uruguay, Cuba. The countries where there are both licensed houses and registration of prostitutes are Albania, Austria, Belgium, France, Greece, Italy, Portugal, Roumania, Spain, Argentina, Chili, Guatemala, French Guinea, Panama, Peru, Salvador, Mexico, Tunis, Morocco, Algeria, Egypt, Turkey, Syria, China, Japan and Siam.**

Most, if not all, the systems of registration and examination are founded upon that which has

* In Queensland prostitutes are medically examined for venereal disease.

** For much of the information respecting the position in regard to the regulations affecting prostitution which are in force in the various countries throughout the civilised world, I am indebted to Miss Alison Neilans's article entitled " Towards Moral Equality: Twenty-five Year's Work and Progress," published in *The Shield* (Vol. v, No. 5).

been in vogue in France for so many generations. There are variations, of course. For instance, in some countries all the prostitutes are inmates of brothels ; in others, while there are no brothels, the women are all compelled to submit to registration and examination.

Of all classes of prostitutes, those who live in brothels are the most slave-like, and, apart from a few old raddled and diseased harlots who infest the poorest parts of the cities, they earn the smallest sums of money. True, the brothel is often a most profitable affair, but little of this profit is garnered by the harlots attached to it. The usual practice is for each girl to receive a percentage of the fees she earns, which are fixed fees and paid to the head of the establishment, usually an aged procurer referred to as the *Madame*. Against these earnings, the girl has to pay for her clothes, perfumes, etc.—costly items, the money for which in the first instance is advanced to her by the management. Often, too, she has to pay for her food. As a rule, in the end, there is little for her to draw, and often she is perpetually in debt to the house. The life is a hard one, as the girl is not allowed any choice as regards the type of men or the number of men she sleeps with—she is compelled to serve all comers and at all times.

In the houses of assignation, which are so numerous in Paris and many other Continental cities, the prostitute is much freer, and usually earns much more money. She is, like the brothel prostitute, in the employment of the management and works on a percentage basis, but she has to be available at certain times only, after which she is free to go to her home.

Many of these brothels and houses of assignation largely rely upon touts to secure clients. These touts are usually chauffeurs, waiters, bartenders, barbers, garage workers and others, who are likely to come into contact with large numbers of men and particularly with commercial travellers and visitors to the city. They work on commission. In many cases a stranger finds it difficult to make the acquaintance of a prostitute except through one of these intermediaries. To anyone familiar with the tactics employed by the women frequenting the West-End of London, and the main streets of many provincial English cities such as Liverpool, Sheffield, Leeds, Cardiff and many others, this statement seems incredible, but nevertheless it is a fact, as those acquainted with Colonial and foreign cities will testify. In most cities which still provide specific " red light districts," whether the brothels are openly conducted or are "underground" affairs, the employment of touts or other intermediaries is a common practice. In certain dubious hotels, such as there are for the finding in most of the larger cities in all countries the world over, there is sometimes an arrangement whereby, on request, girls of easy virtue can be readily secured,

Then there are the registered prostitutes who are not attached to either brothels or houses of assignation. They work on the streets, in the cafe-bars, and the night clubs. All they earn is their own, and, to a certain extent, they are free to pick and choose their men. They are, however, continually harassed in other ways. They must keep within certain specified districts ; they must solicit at certain specified times, and at these times only ; and they are often subjected to demands from the police which are little removed from blackmail.* It is largely from the ranks of these free-lances that the brothel harlots are recruited. A girl falls on bad times, she cannot meet the heavy expenses which her mode of life entails, she is weary of the continual police interference—in sheer desperation she enters a brothel.

The unregistered women are known as clandestine prostitutes. In a country which has a system of licensing, there are not supposed to be any prostitutes other than registered women, but in actual fact there are large numbers who are unregistered.** This is true of every country the world over. It is quite impossible, however stringent are the regulations, however vigilant are the police, to prevent unregistered or clandestine prostitutes from plying their trade. The reasons for this are many. The majority of women do not wish to be branded as prostitutes ; nor do they wish to submit to the indignity and trouble of regular medical inspection. They may wish at some later date to marry, or to enter some other profession ; and the stimga which

* The prevalence of blackmail constitutes one of the major evils in connection with prostitution. The peculiar reaction of society and the law to this particular social phenomenon creates, encourages and develops blackmail. The evil applies in every country, regulationist or non regulationist.

** It may safely be asserted that in all countries where a system of registration is in force the number of clandestine prostitutes is to the number of registered prostitutes as ten is to one.

attaches for life to the registered prostitute is the very thing they are anxious at all costs to avoid.

It is owing to the huge proportion of clandestine harlots that it is impossible to gauge with any pretensions to accuracy the number of prostitutes in any country, any city or any town. The figures issued by various official and social organisations, and which are quoted in books and pamphlets, are mainly guesswork. They are as much guesswork as applied to Paris and other Continental cities where registration is in force, as they are in relation to London or Liverpool or Leeds, where there is no such thing as registration.

It is highly probable that the number of prostitutes fluctuates from time to time in accordance with the prosperity of the country. It is affected, too, by other special circumstances ; such, for instance, as the movements of large bodies of men and the outbreak of war. During the European conflict of 1914-18, the number of prostitutes in French and English cities far exceeded those in evidence at any other time; and for several years after the cessation of hostilities the boom in trade was responsible for much prosperity among the prostitutes of New York, London, Paris, and many smaller cities throughout the world. According to Bishop,* there were in London, immediately before the outbreak of war, some 38,000 professional prostitutes; and at a conservative estimate the close of hostilities would see double that number practising their trade in the capital city. The report of the " Committee of Fourteen," appointed to examine

* Cecil Bishop, *Women and Crime*, Chatto & Windus, 1931.

into conditions in New York City, states that prostitution reached its peak in the year 1928, despite the fact that a campaign against vice had cleared the city of street-walkers and abolished the " red-light " districts. Also prostitutes move from city to city in each country, and from district to district in each city.

Thus, in every case, these women follow the movements of men, whatever may be the reason for men congregating in certain spots. Also prostitutes of certain nationalities show a marked preference for following in the wake of their own countrymen ; in certain cases they are encouraged to do so by the authorities concerned. Thus a government will encourage the emigration of, and, if necessary, will actually provide, women for the use of its nationals in foreign countries.* Chinese prostitutes follow in the tracks of Chinese emigrants ; and similarly with Japanese, Malayan and other races.

Every big city attracts prostitutes because these women are well aware that wherever men foregather in numbers there are potential clients. The fact that in some cities prostitutes may not appear to be present in such profusion or may not parade themselves so blatantly as in others does not mean they are not there for the finding ; it merely means that the bye-laws or regulations are such that soliciting or loitering on the streets would be risky or dangerous. In most cities where soliciting is

---

* Usually this policy is associated with the prohibition of intercourse with native or foreign women, as many men show a preference for women of another nationality.

prevalent, there are certain well-known streets or localities which the prostitutes frequent and where their clients look for them. In instance, the Unter den Linden and the Friedrichstrasse in Berlin ; the St. Pauli district in Hamburg ; the Place Pigalle and the Place Blanche in the Montmartre of Paris ; the Karntnerstrasse in Vienna ; the Altmarkt in Dresden ; the Leicester Square district in London ; the Sixth and Seventh Avenues in the neighbourhood of 42nd Street, New York.

There are, of course, various grades of streetwalkers. The best dressed and the most expensive frequent the more fashionable streets, such as Bond Street and Regent Street. Another and not so expensively upholstered class frequent Wardour Street, Gerrard Street and the adjacent alleys ; a third and lower class are to be found parading in the neighbourhood of the Southampton Street hotels, or near Charing Cross and Victoria stations.

Most of these women intersperse their " streetwalking " with patronage of the drinking-lounges, dance-halls, restaurants and cafés in the districts they favour. Others never solicit on the streets at all, but confine their attentions to the night-clubs and drinking-lounges. Many of these prostitutes are attached to the night-clubs and are allowed free entrance and given a percentage on the sales of drinks, chocolates and cigarettes, which they induce their partners to buy at exorbitant prices. These practices are particularly prevalent in Continental cities, not only in the most expensive night clubs, but in café-bars, dance-halls and drinking saloons. Many of the restaurants in the Champs Elysees, for instance, are frequented by the highest class of prostitute. Similarly, every *nacht lokal* in Berlin is thronged with harlots. So, too, the famous amusement parks, such as the *Volksprata* of Vienna and the Luna Park of Berlin. Many of the so-called dance hostesses are in reality prostitutes practising their profession in camouflaged circumstances.

Naturally the earnings of prostitutes and the fees they charge vary enormously. The cheap harlots who frequent the docks in seaport towns, the East End of London, and the cheaper parts of provincial cities, are often content with a shilling or two and perhaps a glass of beer. A soldier, into whose company I happened to be thrown during the war, who came from a certain Yorkshire industrial town, told me that he had never paid more than a shilling and he had slept with hundreds of women. The girls on the Wardour Street and Gerrard Street beat will ask and get anything from ten shillings to two pounds, according to the age and luxuriousness of the girl, and whether her services are required for the whole night or for a " short time." The Bond Street prostitute will probably turn up her nose at any offer under a couple of pounds.

It is popularly believed that the West End harlots, at any rate, earn a good deal of money, and are able to live in the most prosperous circumstances. This is certainly true of the few. It is not true as regards the majority. There are too many professional prostitutes in the West End of London, as there are in most towns and cities the world over, and competition is extremely keen. It is no unusual thing for a girl to go night after night without earning a penny. And her earnings, when she is in luck, have a habit of dwindling rapidly. It is essential, if she is to be able to charge adequate fees and, in fact, to secure any clients at all, that she must be well-dressed, and often expensively dressed. She has to pay a heavy and often an exorbitant rent, for owners of flats, and landladies letting off rooms, make a " street-walker " pay through the nose.* And there are other incidental expenses, all of which are heavy.

Many of the less prosperous prostitutes, catering almost exclusively for working men, and especially drunken men (incidentally drunken men constitute at least seventy-five per cent. of a prostitute's clients), dispense with flats or rooms. For the carrying on of their trade they make use of dark doorways or passages in unlighted and unfrequented streets, adopting the form of intercourse known as *coitus in statione*. Better-class women, and especially amateur " street-walkers " who have no regular " place of business," often suggest the use of a taxi. The London prostitute's invitation to " come for a taxi-ride, dearie ? " is almost as frequently to be heard on the streets as " will you come to my flat for a little while, darling ? "

A noticeable feature in recent years is the marked number of exceedingly young prostitutes. There is no doubt whatever that to-day prostitutes commence their careers at earlier ages than they did in previous generations. This is doubtless a result of

* In a trial at the Old Bailey in connection with the arranging of " marriages of convenience " between alien women and Englishmen, it was revealed that " flats in the Bond Street area were let to these women at from £6 to £10 a week."

the remarkable precocity of youth which is such a feature of the age we live in.

The young prostitute, provided she is not actually under age, almost invariably possesses an added attractiveness in the eyes of the average man. Few of those looking " for a girl " fail to be tempted by youth or the appearance of youth, and, especially, by virginity. We have seen that in ancient times and among savages, the possession of virginity was not considered to be of any great value and in some cases was to be despised ; but in these civilised days an intact hymen is thought a great deal of by the man who is looking for a *prostitute* to act as a sleeping partner. It is, for one thing, almost a one-hundred per cent. guarantee against venereal infection. For another thing, to many men intercourse with a virgin approximates to marriage. So prized an asset is virginity *in a prostitute* that in brothels the fee demanded in the case of a virgin is invariably considerably higher than that asked for an experienced prostitute. All of which has led to the simulation of virginity, which is by no means so difficult a procedure as would at first sight appear. Often an astringent solution, such as alum, dissolved in water, or vinegar, is used to tighten up the relaxed vaginal walls, and a simulacrum of the virginal haemorrhage is produced by arranging the " deflowering " to occur during the menstrual period. An old trick, mentioned by Erich Wulffen (*Woman as a Sexual Criminal*, Ethnological Press, New York, 1934), which provided the bloody discharge that is expected to accompany defloration, consisted of blistering the vagina by the application

K

of leeches—these blisters, engorged with blood, burst during coitus. The same writer also refers to the surreptitious sprinkling of the sheets with pigeon's blood; an old and favourite method bearing points of resemblance to the ingenious device for providing signs of virginity used in "Mrs. Cole's" eighteenth-century brothel and described in John Cleland's erotic work, *Memoirs of Fanny Hill*. In some cases surgical measures are resorted to, the hymenal opening being reduced to the virginal one-finger dimension by suturing.

There are, in every big city, a few prostitutes who work hand in hand with various types of criminals, notably blackmailers and cardsharpers. After the woman has enticed a client to her room, an "indignant and threatening husband" bursts upon the scene. Eventually, for a monetary consideration, he agrees to overlook the incident. Or the prostitute may introduce her client to some private and exclusive club or other establishment where gaming for high stakes is in progress. Other women make a practice of robbing their clients while they are sleeping, or whenever an opportunity offers. Especially does this apply where the man is drunk. The prostitute has little fear of any charge being brought against her. True, such charges are made occasionally, as the police court reports show, but for every case of robbery where an accusation is lodged against the prostitute who has engineered the robbery, there are a hundred cases where the consequent exposure deters the man from mentioning his loss to anybody, least of all to the police.

CHAPTER XIV

MODERN PRACTITIONERS OF THE OLDEST PROFESSION (continued)—

AMATEUR PROSTITUTES

IN ADDITION to the women who are entirely dependent for their bread and butter on their earnings from the hire of their bodies, there are large and ever-increasing numbers who have other means of earning part or all of their livelihood, and who indulge in promiscuous sexual intercourse as a means of supplementing their incomes. These are prostitutes in all but name. And for the purposes of this work they may be aptly described as amateur prostitutes.

These amateurs for generations have flourished prominently in all big towns and cities. Twenty years ago the shop-girls almost invariably supplemented wages which were insufficient to feed and clothe them adequately, with money earned on the streets. Chorus girls and unstarred actresses, from the days when theatres and music halls were born, secured the bulk of their meretricious finery by just this means.

To-day, true enough, in all walks of life, wages are very much better than in pre-war times. Few girls, from sheer necessity, need walk the streets.

But, paradoxically as it may seem, there are far more amateur prostitutes to-day than there ever were before. They exist in every strata of society, and the fact that these girls would burst into hot anger at the mere suggestion that they were prostituting their bodies, does not alter the fact that they are, in everything except name, morally indistinguishable from the most brazen harlots of Piccadilly.

The reasons for this vast development of amateur prostitution during the last ten years are many. In the first place the desire for smarter clothes and accoutrements has a lot to do with it. Anyone who cares to use his eyes can see, in every city, working girls by the hundred who are dressed in clothes they could not possibly afford if they were dependent solely on their wages. The saying that " men buy their clothes " is as true to-day as it was a quarter of a century ago. The clothes which the girls wear and which the men buy for them are better and smarter—that's the only difference. Then the emancipation of woman, with the concomitant tremendous increase in their freedom, has had a lot to do with it. The decline of parental control over so many young girls has been so great in the past few years that one can justifiably say the girl of to-day enjoys a greater degree of freedom from parental restriction or regulation than did the young man of the same age a couple of decades ago. This freedom is not without its dangers. The sophistication of the youngsters of both sexes, so much talked of in the Press and in social circles, is a sophistication in theory rather than in fact. It must be remembered that it is now fashionable for adolescent girls to be sophisticated, daring, and even vulgar ; just as it is fashionable for them to smoke cigarettes, to drink cocktails, to use lipstick, to avow knowledge of sex and birth control, to discuss obscene literature. Much of this boasted knowledge is erroneous, much more of it is merely silly ; all of it is superficial ; many of the paraded sex adventures are apocryphal. Apart from certain fundamentals, it is questionable whether the young woman of to-day has any more *real* sex knowledge that is of any use to her than had the girl of a previous generation. The difference is that whereas in another age it was the vogue to simulate complete innocence as regards anything remotely connected with sex ; to-day it is the custom to shout any scraps of knowledge one possesses from the house-tops, and to suggest by innuendo an acquaintance with the more tabooed aspects of the sexual credo.

It is easy, as so many modern ignorant parents do, and as the young themselves do, to mistake precocity for knowledge. It is, in fact, this facile confusion, one of the most disturbing and, in a sense, most disgusting, aspects of modern democratic civilisation. Thus, the young modern girl is probably fully convinced that her knowledge of sex, and of all pitfalls connected with it, is adequate. Similarly, modern parents are convinced that their children are " well able to take care of themselves." They are inordinately proud, these parents, of the so-called sex knowledge and moral sophistication of their children ; just as, in another age, they would have been ashamed of these self-same things.

It is here precisely that we touch the danger—a danger all the more pronounced and insidious because both the parents and the children are not only unaware of it but meet with guffaws any suggestion of its existence.

Thus girls, in ever-increasing numbers, are indulging in sexual intercourse before marriage ; so much so, in fact, that the girl who goes to the altar a virgin in any true sense of the word is becoming a rarity. It is true that spectacular evidence of moral guilt, in the shape of unexpected pregnancies, are noticeably less frequent—though even to-day the number of girls who " have to get married " is a very considerable one—but the reason for this lies in the wider acquaintance of men with birth control technique, and the extensive practice of *coitus sine immissio penis*. True enough, girls, too, have more facilities for acquiring birth control information than they ever had before, and there is no doubt that the acquaintance with the technique of contraception which so many of them acquire, gives them confidence and leads them to indulge in sexual adventure to a far greater extent than they would be inclined to do were the fear of pregnancy the bugaboo it once was ; but, despite all this, the man is mainly responsible for the decrease in the number of pregnancies.

Another factor is the entry of women, in such overwhelming numbers, into the business world and into the professions, in competition with men. This has led to an increase in the promiscuity of women, a lowered standard of morals generally, and a decrease in the resistance offered to man's erotic advances. It has led to all these things in two different ways. Before woman's emancipation, as was evident from the inquiry in a preceding chapter, into the reasons for women taking to prostitution as a profession, a girl in any but the peasant class had one profession open to her, and one only, that of marriage. Her whole aim in life was to make a good match ; in other words, to find a man who would provide her with a home for life. For this reason she prized her virginity as she prized a rare and expensive jewel. And it was this very prize which she everlastingly dangled in front of man. To-day marriage is no longer the big and important thing it was. True, most normal girls look upon a successful marriage as the culmination of their careers, but they no longer are obsessed with the urgency and necessity of it, they no longer spend all their waking hours in the rigorous pursuit of it. To the contrary, in most cases, they defer any serious contemplation of marriage until they have had that " good time " which nowadays is on every girl's lips, as at one time it was on every man's. All of which means that, while matrimony is relegated to the shadowy future, sex adventure looms up more importantly than ever. Virginity is laughed at as something terribly old-fashioned.* So much so that those who stress its importance are in danger of being accused of worse practices than normal sexual promiscuity. The modern girl's credo is to drink her fill of enjoyment while she is

---

* Ironically enough, to-day it is the incipient professional prostitute and her client, also pimps and procurers, who attach value to the possession of virginity.

young. To this end she frequents dance-halls, night clubs, restaurants, drinking saloons ; she goes joy-rides with young men whom she scarcely knows from Adam. In other words, she puts herself deliberately and repeatedly into environments and circumstances designed to induce and to develop sexual excitement ; and she indulges increasingly in promiscuous intercourse as the inevitable aftermath.

Often it is the girl who takes the initiative. The seduction of boys, by girls of approximately the same age, is no uncommon occurrence. Mr. Justice Humphreys, commenting upon a case at Wiltshire Assizes, in which a sixteen-year-old boy was charged with a serious offence against a girl aged twelve, according to a report in the *News of the World* (October 7, 1934) said : " Unfortunately, one finds it all over the country, that these young women, whom we used to regard as mere children, are accomplished prostitutes. Many of them go up and invite men to immoral association, and I have no doubt it is true in this case. . . . It is not peculiar to Wiltshire, or the agricultural counties ; it is the same all over England. It is want of parental control and discipline that is at the root of the whole trouble. One of the most painful, horrible things one comes across in these days is the dreadful traits one finds in the female."

Often, through the very fact of entering into man's domain as her profession or business in life, she puts herself, this modern emancipated girl, into circumstances which lead to her seduction. From the beginning of the industrial era, girls who, through force of circumstances, were compelled to leave the shelter of their home, and to earn their livelihood in domestic service, in factories and in shops, have been known to produce from among their ranks the bulk of the prostitutes. It is assumed that the reason for this was the fact that in the past the majority of these girls belonged to the peasant class, and, in consequence, were ignorant, of feeble mentality and unsophisticated. It is a false assumption. The reason for their liability to fall from the path of virtue was in the very fact of having to go out to earn their living, and of being placed in circumstances inimical to the retention of virtue by all except the strong-minded and the ugly. Twenty years ago, almost every shop-girl was a clandestine prostitute. To-day, although the wages paid are such that most girls can live without having recourse to side-lines, the other incidents which lead to seduction and promiscuous sexual relations are not only all present, but they are much more potent. In certain cases the continuance of the girl's position is dependent upon her complacency, in other instances seduction is the price that must be paid to obtain promotion. Every woman is a potential prostitute, just as every man is a potential chaser of prostitutes. It is mainly a question of price, using the word price in a larger and more comprehensive sense than a matter of coin of the realm. The girl who will reject with scorn the proposals of a man belonging to her own station in life, will prove easy prey to the social or stage celebrity ; the lady of title will succumb gleefully to the advances of a prince.

All these causes together are responsible for the fact that to-day more by far than ever before in the world's history, there are for the finding, in every city in Europe and in America, large numbers of girls of respectability who are willing, for all sorts of reasons, to meet men half way in the hunt for sexual excitement and satisfaction. These are the amateur prostitutes of modern civilisation.

The net result of all this is that the professional prostitute's life is becoming an increasingly difficult one. She has to meet the competition of these amateurs, and inevitably, she sees more and more her potential army of clients decreasing. For the average man, on the hunt for sexual adventure, prefers immensely to obtain what he wants from one of these amateurs than from a professional. He always has preferred the amateur to the professional ; the respectable girl to the prostitute. But, until recent years it was impossible for more than a fraction of the men of any country to find girls who were not professional harlots whom they could approach with safety. Always, apart from their comparative rarity, was there the decided risk of these amateurs becoming enciente. Neither the men nor the girls had more than the crudest idea of birth control technique. More and further, there could rarely be anything regular in these orgies with girls of respectability. They were, for the most part, fortuitous affairs, to be taken advantage of when opportunity offered, and not in any sense to be looked upon as providing regular means for the indulgence of libidinous desires. And so, in the overwhelming main, men had to rely upon getting their sexual needs satisfied by the professional prostitute.

There are many reasons why, now that the amateur harlot looms so large on the horizon, men prefer her. For one thing she is cheaper. It is rare that any money is asked for or offered. The girl, in nine cases out of ten, would scorn any such idea. The cost of a drink or two, a theatre seat, a box of chocolates, is usually all that the man is called upon to pay. In many cases he pays nothing at all. But the question of cost is not the main reason which leads the man to prefer the amateur. There are other reasons, compelling reasons, which weigh bigly with him. The most cogent of all, it cannot be too strongly stressed, is the dread fear of venereal disease. There is an idea, so widely disseminated and so firmly established that it is ecumenic as well as axiomatic, that nearly every professional *fille de joie* is afflicted with one of the venereal infections. There is similarly a coincident idea current that the amateur fornicator, who is not considered to be a prostitute at all, is free from infection. Finally, there is the preference which nearly every man has, for a girl who has not been the common property of a number of his kind.

CHAPTER XV

PROSTITUTION AND VENEREAL DISEASE

THE opposition to prostitution is mainly connected with the fear of venereal disease. It is significant that the initiation of the many attempts to stamp out prostitution in Europe were coincident with the outbreak of epidemics of syphilis or gonorrhoea. Before the return of Columbus's expedition and the spreading of a peculiarly virile type of venereal infection throughout Europe, prostitution was either approved or tolerated.

Previous to this time there would appear to have been no connotation made anywhere between prostitution and venereal infection. Medical science, such as it was, had done little investigation into the nature of the diseases now known as syphilis and gonorrhoea.*

It is the contention of some authorities that before the bringing of the infection to Spain by the sailors of Columbus, venereal disease was unknown

---

* Syphilis was first used in reference to venereal disease in 1530, by Fracastoro, in a poem entitled *Syphilis sive Morbus Gallicus*. The bacillus of syphilis was not identified until 1895, when Schaudim named it *Spirochaeta pallida* (now known as *Treponema pallidum*), and shattered for all time John Hunter's thesis that syphilis, gonorrhoea and chancre all resulted from infection with one organism.

in the Old World.* The hypothesis is of the greatest dubiety, and is founded for the most part on the fact that in ancient literature there are no recorded references to syphilis and gonorrhoea specifically as such. But there are references to " the plague " and to the " great pox " ; there are references to " running issues " ; and there is little room for doubt that leprosy was often confounded with syphilis. All things considered, the theory of Gabrul Ayala, quoted by Gluck, wherein he holds that the fifteenth century outbreak was really an epidemic, in a virulent form, of a disease which had existed for centuries, has much to be said for it. In the light of recent trends in the study of the pathology of disease, there is a school of research which more and more inclines to the belief that in the case of most infective diseases a wave of comparative quietude is followed by an epidemical outbreak, the severity of which is in direct ratio to the length of time during which the disease has been latent ; or, alternatively, to the degree of mildness which has characterised its endemic form. The reason advanced in favour of this theory is that every race, in time, develops a degree of immunity to an

* Much of the controversy over the origin of the venereal infections is coloured by moral and religious prejudices ; and there is a tendency for each country to put the blame on some other country. Sanger, in his *History of Prostitution*, asserts that syphilis came to America from Europe, pointing out that the infection was known in England long before the time of Columbus ; as in 1430, some sixty years in advance of the expedition to America, police regulations were put into force in London with the object of prohibiting the entry into brothels of those afflicted with a disease bearing striking points of resemblance to syphilis. In Naples, in 1495, when the city was suffering from a venereal epidemic, the name given to it was " the French malady." It is interesting to note, too, that the condom or sheath, which was invented for use as a venereal prophylactic (not as a birth control device), was, and still is, referred to in England as " French letter " and in France as " *capiton Anglaise*."

infection, and that the more complete is the immunity enjoyed the more severe will be the nature of the attack when a fresh and particularly virile kind of germ is introduced from another country or by another race. An example of this is the recent epidemic of influenza in Europe after many decades of comparative freedom from the disease. In syphilis, in particular, there seems grounds for thinking that racial syphilisation is possible and this provides an explanation for those long periods of apparent quiescence which mark the medical history of civilisation.

Assuming such a hypothesis is the correct one, we can easily discover indications of the presence of venereal diseases as far back as history goes. In the Bible itself there are many references which seem to refer to venereal infections ; in instance, the malady from which the Assyrian king, Esarhaddon, suffered. The pitiable condition of David, described in the 38th Psalm, reads suspiciously like a catalogue of the afflictions of someone suffering from syphilis ; while in the fifteenth chapter of Leviticus there is a description of an affliction that equally suspiciously reads like gonorrhoea ; the plague of Baal-Peor, which carried off 24,000 Israelites might well have been syphilis. Then again, Hippocrates refers to ulcers on the genitals ; Thucydides mentions sores on the sexual organs ; Susruta, in his *Ayurvedas*, describes diseases bearing resemblances to venereal infections, which, three thousand years ago were prevalent in India.

There are scattered references to " ulcers," " sores," and " runnings," in connection with the genitals, through the ages ; and certainly there are references to what seem remarkably like venereal infections long before Columbus made his notable journey to the West Indies. Certainly, too, diseases affecting the genitals were known in England nearly two hundred years before that date. In 1430, there was a London police regulation which excluded from the hospitals any patients suffering from infections which, from their description, bore distinct points of resemblance to venereal diseases. It is this regulation to which, presumably, Sanger refers, in disclaiming that syphilis came to Europe from America.

The full significance of the disease, and the dread fear of it, did not arise however until, as already mentioned, the sailors taking part in the expedition of Columbus, on their return to Europe while suffering from a particularly virile form of syphilis gave the disease to the prostitutes whom they patronised in Barcelona. From Barcelona the infection quickly spread through all the cities of Spain, and thence into France and other countries. So great was the fear of the dread malady that in 1497 an ordnance was passed into law by the Parliament of Paris, whereby any person suffering from the " large pox " was compelled to leave the city within twenty-four hours and to stay away until cured. In this same year, James IV of Scotland was responsible for the banishment from the city of Edinburgh of all venereally infected persons. About the same time, too, Italy was ravaged by syphilis. Cardinals, scholars and nobles alike fell victims to the scourge. Charles VIII was accused of introducing the infection ; Benevenuto Cellini admitted having contracted it from a prostitute ; Sextus della Rovere was " rotten " with it.

These and similar stringent measures for dealing with the infections were adopted in most European countries. No treatment seems to have been given or offered. The infected individuals were treated like so many lepers—driven from their homes or lodgings, they were left to die or to recover according to the whim of God. As the prostitutes were speedily infected and in turn spread the disease among their clients, the outcry against them reached great dimensions, and they were hounded from one city to another. In those days the nature and treatment of the venereal infections were so little understood, that a cure, if it were ever attempted, was rarely effected. Moreover, the prevailing opinion was that any venereal disease constituted God's punishment for the sin of man. This attitude, coupled with the dread fear of infection, resulted in the ostracism of, and lack of any sympathy for, the suffering. Physicians, partly on religious and moral grounds and partly through fear of contracting the infection themselves, for a long time refused to treat venereal disease.

At last, however, when it was demonstrated that venereal infections were almost always contracted through sexual intercourse alone, some crude attempts were made to provide places for the treatment of the malady. In 1505 the French government passed a decree providing for the building of a hospital for persons attacked by the " large pox," but through the opposition of the clergy, it was not

L

until some thirty years later that provision was actually made for the treatment, along with sufferers from other diseases, of those afflicted with syphilis. Even with this much accomplished, the plight of the patients was a pitiable one. The conditions inside the hospital were deplorable, the treatment was of the crudest, and, because of the moral obloquy attached to the infection, every patient suffering from a venereal disease was soundly whipped both on entering and on leaving the establishment.

Towards the close of the seventeenth century, and for some hundred or so years after, we find in France two hospital-prisons in evidence for the treatment of venereal infections ; that of Bicêtre for severe cases and that of Salpétrière for mild infections.

According to contemporary accounts by those in a position to have intimate knowledge of the subject, these hospitals were blots on the civilisation of their day. The conditions under which the poor wretches afflicted with venereal infections were housed and the nature of the treatment meted out to them were alike almost unbelievably bad. It is true that in those days all medical treatment was primitive to a degree, that surgery was of the crudest stamp, and that hygiene was practically unknown. But even so, the physicians and surgeons attached to the hospitals themselves admitted the barbarity of the treatment dispensed to those who were looked down upon as social lepers and outcasts. The wards were badly overcrowded, in each bed several women were compelled to sleep together, the bed-linen was filthy, vermin-infested and often in rags, the food was of the poorest and cheapest procurable and deficient in nutritive qualities. All told, it was a marvel of marvels that any patient ever came out alive. This catalogue of evils was a sufficiently terrible and heartrending one ; but, in addition, the hospital treatment was limited to six weeks' attention, after which, whether better or worse, cured or dying, the patients were bundled out to make room for others ; and, to cap the lot, all the afflicted were compelled to suffer from the distempers with which they were burdened for a full year before they could be admitted.

At this time syphilitic patients, male and female, prostitutes or otherwise, were all treated at these hospitals, or prisons, as they virtually were. Gradually, however, a series of reforms were made; the sexes being segregated, and better treatment and conditions in every way being provided. In 1828 the government decreed that all prostitutes infected with venereal disease should be sent to Saint Lazare, the establishment which, in later years, was to earn notoriety as the prostitute's venereal prison.*

Around the beginning of the eighteenth century, a system of medical inspection was instituted in Germany. Once a fortnight prostitutes were forced to submit to examination and all infected women were detained until cured.

In England, the first serious attempt to provide any form of treatment for the venereally afflicted

---

* At one time as many as 100,000 diseased women were examined in France every year, the majority of whom were sent to prison for treatment.

appears to have been in the reign of Queen Elizabeth. W. Clovves, a surgeon to the Queen, mentions in his writings that syphilis was as prevalent
in England as in any other European country at
that time. He speaks of over a thousand cases of
venereal infection having been treated at St.
Bartholomew's hospital, during a period of five
years.

Later, the Lock Hospital, Southwark, founded,
according to Acton, " on the site of a house for
lepers," specialised in the treatment of the venereally
afflicted. This hospital, which was largely kept up
by private subscription, found it advisable to
camouflage its real work. Acton, writing in 1857,
says : " It would almost seem to one reading the
annual report of the charity, that the governing
body are painfully nervous lest its real aim should
appear in black and white upon their pages."*

This would appear to have been in keeping with
the policy of avoiding any mention of the venereal
infections by their real names, which policy prevailed during the whole of the nineteenth century,
and, in certain circles, prevails to this day.** Thus
syphilis and gonorrhoea were invariably referred
to as " social diseases " or " blood poison " or
" bad sickness " ; brothels were dubbed " houses
of ill-fame " or " sporting-houses " ; prostitutes

* William Acton, *Prostitution, Considered in its Moral, Social and Sanitary
Aspects*, Churchill, 1857, p. 135.

** It is true that since the war a remarkable change has taken place in
respect to the terminology employed by the public and by writers in
contemporary novels. But this applies to expletives, vulgarisms and
slang, rather than to the language of venery. The Press rarely refers to
sexual matters in any but euphemized terminology ; it still refers to
pregnancy or parturition as " an interesting event."

themselves were described as " fallen women " or
" gay ladies."

Meanwhile, in various European countries, as
all attempts to suppress prostitution by punishment, imprisonment, segregation and exile, had
completely failed, and the prevalence of venereal
disease showed no sign whatever of abating, the
thoughts of the governments centred more and
more on the medical inspection of prostitutes. It
was found impossible to drive the women, diseased
or otherwise, out of the cities. It was equally
impossible, even with the provision of hospitals for
the treatment of venereal diseases, to get those
afflicted to attend these hospitals of their own free
will. The only solution, it was argued, lay in making
attendance compulsory. To do this entailed the
rigorous observance of two regulations. All prostitutes must be registered, and all must be medically
examined at frequent and regular intervals. As
we have seen in our examination, many Continental
countries adopted this system of registration and
compulsory medical inspection. But others, notably
Great Britain, refused to adopt any such system ;
the opponents of regulation basing their case
mainly on the contention that the licensing of
prostitutes implied the licensing of vice and was
indefensible on moral and religious grounds. But
I shall deal with the pros and cons of regulation in
another and subsequent chapter.

With the failure, now generally admitted among
those who have given to the subject careful study,
of all methods of combating venereal disease by a
system of medical examination restricted to prosti-

tutes, in recent years the problem has been approached in other ways. In certain of the British colonies, notably Australia, Canada, New Zealand, and South Africa, venereal diseases are classed as infectious diseases, and notification and treatment are stated to be compulsory. It is, however, one thing to make a disease notifiable and treatment compulsory ; it is quite another thing to enforce such an Act. Those who advocate these measures, and there are in every country many who favour their adoption, overlook the fact that there is no point of comparison between a venereal infection and an infectious disease such as typhoid, or small pox, or diphtheria. One might just as well pass an Act branding constipation, or colic, or acne, or lumbago as a notifiable disease. The net result of making venereal disease notifiable is to cause the majority of the afflicted to take elaborate precautions against the discovery of their condition, even to the extent of eschewing medical advice and in its stead attempting self-treatment.* It must be remembered that the concealment of a dose of gonorrhoea or of syphilis, at any rate in its early stages, presents no difficulties whatever. Neither of these infections indisposes the party afflicted. Indeed many women suffer from gonorrhoea and do not know it. In view of all this, therefore, one need feel no surprise that at a Canadian conference held in 1931 it was admitted that there was no evidence of a fall in the

---

* Even when those afflicted with venereal disease are discovered and reported by doctors or others to the authorities, in numerous cases they disappear and cannot be traced. In other instances fictitious addresses are given. Again, many doctors do not carry out the provisions of the Act by reporting cases to the Medical Officer of Health.

incidence of venereal disease since compulsory
notification was introduced. Similarly at a Medical
Conference of the Commonwealth and States of
Australia held in 1922, it was admitted that
" private patients do not get notified," and there
was " no evidence to show that the passing of this
legislation has resulted in any reduction of the
prevalence of congenital venereal infections." The
available evidence seems to support the contention
that the compulsory system fails dismally in any
true sense. Its application is necessarily restricted
to certain sections of the population, such as
criminals, beggars, workhouse inmates, and hospital
patients.

In Great Britain there is in force a voluntary
system of treatment for those infected with venereal
disease.* Free clinics are provided in many towns
and cities, where patients may be treated. There
are 188 of these centres or clinics, and, according
to the official figures, at these centres, during the
year 1932, a total of 14,167 cases were dealt with
for the first time. These figures tell their own tale.
They include all three venereal infections, and it is
surely too much to believe that out of the millions
of men and women running the risk of venereal
infection during the year, only some 14,000 become
infected. Clearly these cases constitute but a fraction of the venereally diseased in the country. The
failure of the scheme, for failure it is, is due to the
fact that comparitively few people are prepared to
advertise to the world that they are suffering from

* In Sweden a compulsory system of treating venereal disease is in force.

a venereal infection.*   It is true that the *treatment* is given in privacy, but, as in all cases of anything securable through governmental or official bodies, before the treatment can be obtained, there is a long period of waiting to be endured. This period of waiting is passed in a public room and at a certain specified time—these stipulatory conditions suffice to advertise the patient's infection as thoroughly as if his name and ailment were pla-carded on a public notice-board. Thus, of the infected, relatively few present themselves for treatment. In addition, those who do make an initial visit to a clinic, rarely continue their attend-ances until thoroughly cured. The moment the outward signs of the disease have vanished they cease to attend.**

One other scheme for dealing with the menace of venereal disease must be mentioned. Despairing of any method of preventing prostitutes from infecting the men,*** during the world war, when the incidence of venereal disease was so high that the authorities became alarmed, attention was

* Euphemistic names for venereal disease are adopted by doctors and their patients. Cases of gonorrhoeal arthritis are referred to as rheumatism ; gonorrhoeal vesiculitis is recorded as peritonitis or appendicitis ; G.P.I., which so often is the aftermath of long-standing syphilitic infection, is described as paresis, or dementia paralytica or softening of the brain ; cerebral haemorrhage, caused by syphilis, is nearly always called apoplexy or " a stroke."

** The international scheme, known as " The Brussels Agreement," for the treatment of seamen afflicted with venereal disease, has largely failed for similar reasons. This Agreement, made in 1924, enables all merchant seamen and watermen of any nationality to be given free medical treatment at clinics provided at various ports.

*** Soldiers on active service, in considerable numbers, so far from avoiding infection, welcomed it. In giving evidence before the Special turned towards the male. The men were instructed in the technique of venereal prophylaxis, and they were supplied with the necessary materials for self-disinfection. Practically all the armies adopted this plan during the years of war, though there was a good deal of dispute as to its efficacy. Although prophylaxis has never been made available to the civil population, it is evidently still largely relied upon to keep down the incidence of venereal disease in the forces, for, as recently as 1930, a question in Parliament respecting the provision of " pocket anti-venereal outfits, or prophylactic packets for self-disinfection," in the Navy, elicited the statement that it was " proposed to continue to provide such facilities for the voluntary use of naval personnel " ; but that lectures are given conveying warnings respecting the dangers connected with " promiscuous sexual intercourse " and " no coercion is employed to induce men to make use of these facilities."

The incidence of venereal disease, in the forces as the published figures establish, certainly shows a

Committee on Venereal Disease appointed by the Birth Rate Commission, Miss Ettie A. Rout (Hon. Secretary, New Zealand Volunteer Sisters) stated it to be a fact that prostitutes suffering from venereal disease could command a higher fee than those free from disease. In considering the conflicting evidence relative to the efficacy of venereal prophylaxis, this point, that the men did not wish to avoid an infection, must not be overlooked. In her evidence Miss Rout said : " Some men wanted to get diseased during the War. They would sell the discharge to other men and they would infect their genital organs with it. Some infected their eyes and came in blind." In reply to a question, " If people are going to do that to avoid the firing line, prophylaxis will not be of use ? " the witness stated : " That is where the failure came in ; it accounted for one-third of the Paris leave infections," *Prevention of Venereal Disease,* Williams & Norgate, 1921, pp. 91-2.

steady and considerable decrease,* but whether this decrease is wholly or partly or in any sense due to prophylaxis, is a debatable point.

Certainly there can be no question that calomel ointment applied at the *proper time and in the right way* will prevent syphilitic infection ; and that, in the majority of cases, permanganate of potassium, also applied at the *proper time and in the right way*, will prevent gonorrhoea. But the trouble is that few men will apply chemical prophylaxis with sufficient care. In many cases, through drink, they are incapable of carrying out the essential technique at all. To be effective, prophylaxis must be done within an hour of exposure to infection ; the ointment in the one case, and the solution in the other, must be applied thoroughly and carefully. More, the prophylaxis must be repeated after every act of coitus or attempted act of coitus. Often there are no proper facilities for self-disinfection ; often the man is careless ; often he does it only half-heartedly;

* The figures for 1921 and 1931, showing the decrease in the decade under review, are as under :

ARMY.

(Cases ratio per 1,000 strength.)

			Gonorrhoea.	Syphilis.	Soft chancre.	Total
1921	..	..	45.9	15.6	12.5	74.0
1931	..	..	21.5	4.5	4.8	30.8

NAVY.

(Cases ratio per 1,000 strength.)

			Gonorrhoea.	Syphilis.	Soft chancre.	Total.
1921	..	..	71.38	26.48	15.42	113.28
1931	..	..	51.59	7.49	9.84	68.92

AIR FORCE.

(Cases ratio per 1,000 strength.)

			Gonorrhoea.	Syphilis.	Soft chancre.	Total.
1921	..	..	26.2	8.0	1.9	36.1
1931	..	..	10.8	2.1	1.7	14.7

I am indebted for these statistics to the *Empire Social Hygiene Year Book*, 1934 ; Allen & Unwin.

often he intends doing it but neglects or forgets until it is too late. Actually, the condom (" French letter ") is a far more efficient prophylactic for the huge majority of men than is any chemical method available to them.

There can be no doubt, too, that the mere fact of being in possession of a prophylactic packet causes a man to take risks which, in other circumstances, he would hesitate to incur. It is true that lectures are given on the dangers of " promiscuous sexual intercourse," but such lectures are robbed of any value they might otherwise possess by the provision, coincidentally, of venereal prophylactics. You cannot tell a man on Saturday how to avoid the evil results of pleasurable vice, and on Sunday expect him to take much notice of a moral lecture against the practice of that vice.

It is the eternal conflict between morals and health* which has led to the refusal to supply the civil population with the facilities for venereal prophylaxis that are so freely given to men in the forces. It is this same deference to morals and religion that has led the government to prohibit the selling of prophylactics (as such) to the public, or the provision of information regarding prophylaxis by anyone other than a medical practitioner.**

* This conflict has always been with us. The bulk of the public still looks upon the venereal infections as God's punishment for the sins of immorality, and the hospital wards in which cases are treated are known in many cases as " foul " wards.

** There is no law against anyone purchasing the chemicals employed in venereal prophylaxis, provided they are bought as chemicals and not as venereal prophylactics ; and there is no law against the chemist selling these chemicals, provided he does not sell them specifically as prophylactics or give instructions as to their use for this purpose. Similarly, there is no law against the sale and purchase of the most widely used mechanical prophylactic in the world.

True, there are many reasons which could be brought forward against the sale of chemical prophylactics, the principal of which is that they create a false sense of security, but the reason behind the policy of the government is merely a pandering to moralistic intolerance and superstition.

We now come to the question of whether or not venereal disease is more prevalent among prostitutes than among respectable members of the population ? In dealing with venereal disease, the great difficulty is to obtain any figures that can be conceded to be in any way reliable. The social obloquy attached to any admission of infection is so great even today that most men and women go to any lengths, adopt any subterfuge, and lie like troopers, rather than admit that they are afflicted, or ever have been afflicted, with venereal disease. The State and the medical profession aid and abet the policy of evasion and camouflage. Except in regard to inmates of prisons, workhouses and asylums, deaths from syphilis or gonorrhoea are never signified as such on death certificates ; terms such as apoplexy and peritonitis being employed. It is for this reason that the idea has got abroad that criminals, lunatics, prostitutes, *et al* are more afflicted with venereal disease than are any other classes of society. There are grounds for assuming that, popular opinion notwithstanding, prostitutes are less likely to be infected than are many of the so-called girls of respectability and a goodly number of married women. Professional prostitutes, for the most part, in these days, take great care to avoid infection. It is a serious matter for a prostitute, registered or unregistered, to become infected, admitting that she can often and, at any rate, for some time, prevent her condition being known even to a medical man. Many prostitutes patrolling the West End of London insist upon the man using a prophylactic—they go so far as to carry in their handbags and to keep in their flats supplies of these mechanical preventives of infection. In addition, a very considerable proportion of these women themselves use a chemical prophylactic, even though it may be a somewhat crude one. Now, the majority of amateur prostitutes neither adopt themselves, nor insist upon their partner adopting, any protective measure at all—in the main they have no knowledge of prophylaxis. The minority who do know something of venereal prophylaxis, with scarcely an exception, leave the matter to the man. Married women, similarly, know little or nothing of these things, and it is a safe assumption that there are more respectably married women infected with syphilis and gonorrhoea every year than there are professional harlots so infected. The bulk of the prostitutes who suffer from venereal infections are the cheap low-class women who frequent the poorer parts of the cities, and, especially, the docks of seaport towns.

There is another reason why the incidence of venereal disease is relatively lower in the ranks of professional prostitutes than among amateurs and women of respectability. After years of practice in her profession the harlot often acquires a certain degree of immunity to infection.

The question of venereal disease and its prophylaxis is to some extent connected with the abnormally low fertility rate among prostitutes. It is well known that prostitutes give birth to relatively few children, and this applies to all ranks of the profession. A good proportion of the men who visit professional women use condoms, and in this way venereal prophylaxis acts incidentally as a contraceptive practice. Then, too, many prostitutes are in the habit of adopting every available precaution against conception. It is true that because of the demands made by their clients, in many cases, some of the more efficacious birth control methods are denied them, but nearly all use vaseline liberally, in addition to antiseptic douches and sponging. Japanese prostitutes are adepts at " wiping-out " the vagina with the finger wrapped with cotton or rice paper and dipped into an antiseptic solution. Abortion, too, is common. In some cases it is self-induced by the use of strong purgatives and emmenagogues as well as mechanical interference ; but even more of it is caused by excessive indulgence in coitus ; by pathological conditions of the vagina, cervix and uterus ; and by sterility induced through long-standing gonorrhoea.

CHAPTER XVI

THE TRAFFIC IN WOMEN

ONE outcome of modern brothel prostitution is what is generally and popularly known as " white slave traffic." Everybody who reads the news-papers has heard of " white slavery," and most people have gathered a grossly exaggerated idea as to its extent. As a result of reading the lurid accounts in the sensational Press, there are those who immediately jump to the conclusion that every girl or young woman who disappears from her home has been carried off forcibly by the monsters in human form which throng the streets of London on the look-out for girls to kidnap.

The term " white slave traffic " is a misnomer. Not by any means all the girls who are inveigled into becoming brothel prostitutes or mistresses, belong to the white races. In the East the brothels are thronged with women of every shade of black and yellow ; and these girls of colour are searched for by those engaged in the business of prostitution with the same diligence as are girls flourishing paler skins.

As far as white women are concerned, the bulk of them are shipped to the Argentine and other South American States ; and to Shanghai, where there is a big and steady demand for young girls of all European races.

The reasons for this demand are many. In every country in the world where the number of males is largely in excess of the number of females, either permanently or temporarily, the demand for prostitutes is a considerable one. In newly-settled countries and in other spots where, for any reason whatever, women are in the minority, does this apply. Thus the demand may shift from one place to another in accordance with the movements of men. This is well exemplified in the case of troops moving from one country to another. Wherever there is such movement, there is a demand for women. In the case of soldiers the demand is for the cheaper type of prostitute. Countries, too, which attract tourists in any quantity are suitable places for the opening of brothels, and call for the importation of foreign prostitutes.* Then again the erotic requirements of wealthy men, even where the shortage of women is not a particularly noticeable feature, is a factor not to be overlooked. These men are constantly requiring fresh mistresses. As the charms of one girl wear off, a new mistress is called for. And some men have a strong predilection for virgins. Then again, there are men willing to pay phenomenally high prices for girls or women who are willing to be parties to perverse sexual practices. They prefer, too, in many cases, women of a foreign race. Inevitably is there an added

---

* According to the League of Nations' Report, Egypt, Algiers, and Tunis, being tourist centres, are supplied with prostitutes by the traffickers. " The *madame* of a house of prostitution in Algiers admitted that inmates from Parisian houses were sent there at the seasons of the year when it was frequented by tourists."—*Report of the Special Body of Experts on Traffic in Women and Children*, Part One, p. 14.

incentive where novelty can be added to the basic allurement of sex.

Even where the supply of native women may be adequate, it is often difficult to fill the brothels with girls of a type which the clients of these brothels require. In *all countries* having brothels and a licensing system, with or without medical inspection, it is becoming increasingly difficult to obtain recruits in sufficient numbers from among the native population. The conditions of life in these brothels, the poor remuneration, and other drawbacks, cause girls more and more to engage in free-lance prostitution ; and, in countries where free-lance prostitution is not allowed, to elude registration as long as possible. In consequence, in brothels which rely upon recruiting their inmates from the local population they have to be content, in the majority of cases, with the lowest type of harlot. Often these brothels are peopled with raddled old whores. The only way to secure the services of pretty young girls is for the owners to get into their clutches foreign girls.

There is, too, yet another reason which applies in certain countries where the bulk of the prostitutes are aliens ; a reason which not only leads to the retention of a system which encourages the importation of foreign women, but also prevents any measures being taken to deport such women as have entered the country.* This reason is simply that the governments of these countries consider

* Deportation of alien women is one of the methods of combating the traffic in women recommended by the League of Nations Investigation Committee.

M

the employment of foreign prostitutes affords a considerable degree of protection to their own girls and women.

The brothels of Buenos Ayres, Shanghai, and other cities are always looking for European women suitable for their purpose.* Their clients are men of considerable wealth who will pay handsomely for youth and prettiness, and who tire so quickly of any one girl that they are everlastingly seeking fresh charmers. Usually a girl, after acting as a sort of temporary mistress to a wealthy client, is returned to the brothel and thence, stage by stage, sinks into the position of common prostitute. By the time the girl's freshness has worn off she has proved a most remunerative investment to the trafficker.

The business is highly organised and gives employment to a number of intermediaries, all of whom have to earn their livings in one way or another out of the girls whom they provide for the enjoyment of the brothel patrons. There are the *souteneurs*,** or other agents, who procure the girls in the first instance, and in some cases live on them ; there are the *madames*,*** who manage the brothels into which the girls are placed ; and there are the owners, who provide the capital for the establishment of the brothels and the procuration of the

* According to the League of Nations Report, it is estimated there are at least 4,500 foreign prostitutes in Buenos Ayres.

** *Souteneur*—a pimp. Also referred to as " Bully " or " ponce " (England), " *Zuhalter* " (Germany), " cadet " (America). Not every pimp is a procurer. The term is applied to a very large number of men connected with prostitution, including those who live on the earnings of prostitutes ; and those who act as procurers for brothels.

*** A *madame* has usually herself been a prostitute and knows every phase of the profession.

girls, but who rarely appear on the actual scene of operation.

Now, despite the sensational stories which are current respecting the number of innocent girls lured from their homes by the " white slave " traffickers, the bulk of the recruits secured are already engaged in prostitution, either as fully-fledged professional harlots or as amateurs. And, even of these, the professional women outnumber the amateurs by ten to one. The reasons which cause professional prostitutes to throw in their lot with the *souteneurs* who approach them are many. One compelling reason is the promise of big earnings in the South American or Eastern brothels, or the chance of becoming the temporary mistress of some wealthy business man. Especially does this prospect appeal to the inmate of a European brothel, where the earnings are probably microscopic. Again, in the case of a free-lance prostitute, the continual pressure of police interference, the diffi-culty experienced in earning a living, or any one of a dozen other reasons, may cause her to embrace with glee the prospect of entering a brothel in a foreign country and, especially, in one which is presented to her as a Golconda.

The amateur prostitute often falls for the bait offered by the experienced *souteneur*, only here he is not quite so sure of his ground. It is becoming increasingly difficult to distinguish between the girl who, in all but name, is a " street-walker," and the one who is merely out for a good time and would jib at the notion of becoming a professional prosti-tute. With the amateur, therefore, the agent adopts a different method. He takes the girl to the theatre, to the cinema, to dance halls and to restaurants, gives her presents, and acts the part of the wealthy man about town. Eventually he suggests a foreign trip, and usually the bait is swallowed. This method is *sometimes* adopted and occasionally proves successful in the case of respectable girls of poor parentage or orphans, who are working in London or some other city far removed from their homes. With girls of these types, if every other plan fails, marriage, bogus or real, overcomes every difficulty.

Chorus girls and artistes attached to low-grade theatres and touring companies, and the hordes of girls of every kind who are anxious to get on the stage, provide a certain number of recruits. It is not difficult for a skilled *souteneur*, posing as a producer or a theatrical agent looking for likely talent for Continental shows, to induce inexperienced girls to go abroad on these pretences. In many cases the girls are given jobs as dancers, singers or entertainers at cabarets which are really brothels, and sooner or later they are compelled to prostitute themselves. The first step taken, it is not long before they become brothel prostitutes in every sense of the word.

Although, in most countries, there are stringent laws against the employment abroad of girls under twenty-one years of age, the traffickers succeed in getting a good number of " underweights," as they are called.* They falsify the papers, and instruct

* In some cases girls secure entry into a country as stowaways.

the girls to swear, when questioned, to being over twenty-one.

With a negligible number of exceptions, these girls who become " white slaves " do so voluntarily, and even where they may not be exactly aware of the precise nature of their proposed employment, they have a tolerably good idea that promiscuity and immorality are part of the duties expected of them. The bulk of these girls, for one reason or another, are in difficulties. Their difficulties may be of many kinds, through lack of money or prospects of securing employment of a kind they will accept, are the predominating motives. Even the prostitutes who are recruited for service in foreign brothels are mainly in distress—the *successful* free-lance prostitute would spit in the face of any trafficker who made overtures to her.

Summed up, it is a relatively safe assumption that ninety-five per cent. of the girls recruited for work in brothels have already had some experience of promiscuity ; and of the remainder, four per cent. are not unwilling to give it a trial. The traffickers are not keen upon recruiting girls who are likely to give them a deal of bother, and who, even when they are lured into a brothel, have to be raped by the clients. Few men, despite the sensational stories related in the Press, in novels, and in pamphlets published for purely propagandistic purposes, are enamoured of girls, however pretty they may be, who reject every advance and whose surrender entails the employment of force. For all these reasons the cases of kidnapping or abduction of girls for the purposes of prostitution, *against their will*, are rare.

If a young prostitute, professional or amateur, can be induced to leave her own country, she becomes a mere tool in the capable hands of those whose business it is to exploit her. Usually the girl works on a commission basis, but out of this commission she has to pay for clothes, food, perfumes, doctor's fees, and graft to the police. In most cases she is constantly in debt to the *madame* who runs the brothel. It is part of the *madame's* policy to see that the girls are indebted to her, as this gives her power over them.

Apart from fluctuations due to the movements of bodies of men, and changing conditions, the one country which, in the past twenty years, has provided the biggest scope for traffic in women is, without question, the Argentine Republic. Brazil, Uruguay, the Panama, Mexico, and Egypt also take considerable numbers of women. But overshadowing all these, and ranking next in importance to the Argentine, as a market for white women, is Shanghai. Moreover Shanghai presents a rapidly growing market. The huge Chinese and considerable cosmopolitan population of this city seem to have an insatiable appetite for prostitutes ; and it is a noteworthy, and at the same time a disturbing fact, that the coloured men, in constantly growing numbers, prefer *white women*. To Shanghai, then, there is a stream of women—women of every white race and nationality, though at the moment Russians predominate. To other Chinese and Eastern cities, too, these white women, in ever-increasing numbers, are migrating. This movement is perhaps the most alarming and significant point in connection with recent trends in the traffic in women.

So, in one guise or another, women are drawn to the cities of the Argentine, to Shanghai, and to other places, from every European country. Even England supplies a certain number, though, owing to the extra difficulties which are experienced in getting girls out of this country, the proportion of British-born recruits, in comparison with those of other nationalities, is relatively small. But, difficult as it undoubtedly is to pilot a girl past the British emigration officials, it is not an impossible feat. The practice, during recent years, of allowing those travelling to certain Continental ports on day-trips to dispense with a passport, has facilitated greatly the task of the agents engaged in securing recruits. It is not by any means a difficult matter for a *souteneur* and his " wife " to make the acquaintance of a pretty unattached girl, and to get her to accompany them on a trip to France. Once on French soil, the administration of a few drops of chloral hydrate solution* and the girl knows nothing until next morning she wakes up in a bedroom with a strange man. She is compromised, she is helpless, she probably has no acquaintance with the language. The rest is easy.

All the seaside resorts, and especially Brighton and Blackpool, are favourite hunting grounds for these *souteneurs*. After a few days in France, the

---

* Known in the underworld as " knock-out drops."

recruits are shipped from Marseilles—the world's most notorious centre for " white slave " traders—to the Argentine and other places.

In some cases the girl does not go into a brothel at all. She works for the *souteneur*, turning over to him the money she earns. There are cases of this kind in every large city the world over ; and although, in many countries, it is a criminal offence for a man to live on the immoral earnings of a woman, the number of prosecutions bears no relation whatever to the number of actual instances where this arrangement between a prostitute and her man holds. The difficulty is to secure evidence for a conviction. The prostitute can rarely be induced to give evidence. For in nearly every case she prefers the arrangement ; often it is of her own seeking.

The relation between prostitute and *souteneur* or bully, as he is termed in England, has often proved a puzzle to sociological students. It seems strange that any woman will be willing to prostitute her body in order to keep a man in idleness, who, often enough, is not married to her; especially as it is a well-known fact that these bullies are often cruel to their women. It is held by many that the explanation lies in the fact that the bullies in reality are the lovers of the prostitutes who work for them, supplying the psychological factor that is lacking in their clients, and that the attachment of the prostitute to her lover is close and deep. Other observers contend that the true explanation lies in fear. These bullies are cruel, callous criminals who will stop at nothing, and the women who have got into their clutches are afraid to leave them, just as much as they are afraid to give them away to the police. Now, I have no doubt both these explanations possess some atom of truth, but they by no means reveal the whole or indeed the main truth. The bully is the woman's protector. Prostitutes are human, like other women. Not all of them are the brass-faced, hard-mouthed harridans popular opinion personifies ; many, even in the lower ranks of the profession, are nothing like a match in hardness, vindictiveness and unscrupulousness for their clients. There are in existence, and in considerable numbers, too, men who do not hesitate to decamp without paying the fee agreed upon. The prostitute cannot invoke the aid of the law in the securing of her just dues. She is socially ostracised, and her word would count for nothing against that of a so-called respectable member of society. It is for these reasons that she often finds a bully, upon whom she can rely to put in an appearance when called upon, to accord her psychical as well as physical protection, to negotiate on her behalf with landlords, owners of flats, hotel-keepers, and in other business deals ; a most valuable aid in the pursuit of her profession. Also there are a number of young, inexperienced and unintelligent prostitutes who not only learn to lean upon some man to look after them, but who would be helpless without guidance. These are the girls who are handed from pimp to pimp, or from brothel to brothel, like so many pieces of merchandise. They are bullied and trampled upon hope-

170 A HISTORY OF PROSTITUTION

lessly. They have no knowledge of their rights as human beings ; they have no notion of rebellion.

Mixed up with the traffic in women is the traffic in drugs and in obscene literature and pictures. Both drugs and obscene publications are sold in brothels at exorbitant prices. Pictures illustrating every form of sexual perversity are part of the stock in trade of many prostitutes.*

Most of the girls who are recruited into the trade, even by false pretences, continue to work as prostitutes for some time. They do not leave the profession at the first opportunity. The popular idea, fanned by sensational accounts in the Press, in novels and on the films, that these " white slaves " are virtually prisoners and cannot escape, once they are " within the toils," is nonsense. Even allowing for the difficulties occasioned through being in a foreign country, with the language of which they are unfamiliar, they are not kept inside a prison cell or guarded. They could escape if they wanted to, and there is usually a representative of their own country to whom an appeal could be made. The fact that they put up with their lot is significant. And the reason they put up with their lot is, unless I greatly err, that they can see no other way of earning a living, that they care to adopt.

All warnings issued by governments, by moralists, by social workers and by others, against entering the profession of prostitution have proved unavailing.

* Free-lance prostitutes themselves are buyers of obscene literature and pictures. They find these provide additional attractions for their clients, and a man will often go home with a girl who can offer him such like excitants of his sexual appetite. Many of the London " street-girls " in soliciting stress the fact that they have " naughty books and pictures " in their flats.

You cannot put down vice by warning people against it. Every warning against vice is an advertisement for vice.

Attempts to suppress the traffic in women by legislative and other remedial measures have only proved partially successful. The chronicle of the campaign provides an interesting chapter in the history of the conflict against vice. Attention was first brought to the fact that English girls were being utilised in Continental brothels, during the movement for the repeal of the Contagious Diseases Acts of 1864, 1866, and 1869. A government inquiry was made, and, as a result of this inquiry, the Criminal Law Amendment Act of 1885, which included a section specifically designed to deal with procuration, made it a severe offence to procure for the purposes of unlawful carnal intercourse any female under the age of twenty-one years.

To a certain extent this Act reduced the traffic, but it did not eliminate it. And " white slavery " still loomed large in the eyes of the public, and was made much of in the " stunt " Press. By the year 1904, the movement against the " white slave traffic," sponsored in England by Alexander Coote, and in France by Senator Berenger, became an international affair, and some years later, to be precise in 1910, thirteen nations,* the delegates of which met at an International Convention for the Suppression of White Slave Traffic, agreed to make the procuration of women and girls punishable in

* The nations concerned were Austria-Hungary, Belgium, Brazil, Denmark, France, Germany, Great Britain, Italy, The Netherlands, Portugal, Russia, Spain and Sweden.

each country concerned. Then, before much progress was made, came the European War, and with nearly every country's energies concentrated in the conflict, such comparatively trivial matters were forgotten.

The next important step in the campaign against procuration was the movement initiated by the League of Nations. When the League was formed, one of the Articles of its constitution provided for the entrusting of the League " with the general supervision over the execution of agreements with regard to the traffic in women and children." Eventually a body of experts were appointed to make a thorough investigation of the position, and the results of this investigation have been published in a series of voluminous reports.

From the mass of statistical and other information contained in these reports, one big fact stands out prominently and durably, to wit, that the traffic in women is inextricably mixed up with and centred in the system where the licensing of brothels is in vogue. These brothels represent the trafficker's market ; without them those who export women would be forced out of business. All attempts to reduce or exterminate the traffic in women must concentrate upon the abolition of brothels and the prevention of third-party profit in prostitution. The Report states :

" The existence of licensed houses is undoubtedly an incentive to traffic both national and international. The fact has been established by previous enquiries and is admitted to be true by many Governments as a result of their experience.

The enquiries made by us not only confirm this fact but show, as other observers have remarked, that the licensed house becomes in some countries the centre of all forms of depravity. These establishments constantly require more inmates to replace those who leave and to meet the desires of their clients for change."*

Other measures which the Commission recommended as effective in curtailing or preventing the traffic, include the strict supervision of agencies for foreign employment ; the deportation of foreign prostitutes, *souteneurs*, and traffickers ; the introduction of penalties in cases where it can be proved that *souteneurs* are marrying their victims in order to evade emigration restrictions ; and a strengthening or tightening up of the laws dealing with those who live upon the earnings of prostitutes.

It is, however, one thing to recommend ; it is entirely another thing to get the recommendations adopted. It is yet another thing to *enforce* the carrying out of such recommendations even when they are adopted. The difficulty is big enough where one country only is concerned ; it is well-nigh insurmountable where practically the whole world is concerned.

For the League's recommendations to be effective it would require all nations to agree to them and to carry them out ; a difficulty which is just as insurmountable in the case of so amorphous a matter as morals as it has proved to be in the question of war. Different countries view such things as promiscuity

* *Report of the Special Body of Experts on Traffic in Women and Children*, Part One, 1927, p. 47.

in very different ways. In instance, prostitution is widespread in China, Japan and other Eastern countries, as the recent League of Nations Inquiry has revealed, and what is looked upon as so shameful a trade in Western civilisation ranks as a legitimate profession among Eastern peoples.

Then again, even in those countries which are agreed as to the measures to be taken, difficulties are apparently experienced in carrying out these measures. Thus in 1921 a number of nations agreed to punish all traffic in women under the age of twenty-one. One of these countries was France ; and yet we find, according to the Report for 1927, that of the registered prostitutes in Paris almost one-third were under twenty-one years of age.

Yet again when the question of punishing the traffic in women *of any age* was raised, a number of countries refused to agree to this. And so it goes on.

What it all amounts to is that while *all governments* agree that the prostitution of women *in other countries* is an evil to be attacked with every weapon possible, many are inclined to take an entirely different view of prostitution *in their own country*.

There is, in the Commission's Report, a significant admission that all the recommendations made " are not likely to be successful while the incentive of money-making remains. Profit is at the bottom of the business." It is because of this that the Commission stresses the importance of punishing the " *souteneurs, madames* and others, who live on the proceeds of prostitution." Punishment, *per se*, however, will not stop the traffic, any more than punishment in past ages stopped prostitution itself.

The real root of the trouble lies deeper than this. It lies in the causes which induce the *woman* to prostitute her body. So long as women can be obtained, by any means short of actual kidnapping, there will be found men and women willing to undergo the risks connected with the traffic, and skilful enough to devise means of evading every regulation, in return for the handsome profits to be made out of the business.

The root cause, from the woman's standpoint, as I have pointed out in another chapter of this work, is *relative poverty*. This factor, the League of Nations would seem to have overlooked. Without the removal of this fundamental cause, which resolves itself into an economic problem of major importance, all other measures, useful as they may be in a supplementary sense or as palliatives, are essentially futile.

CHAPTER XVII

MALE PROSTITUTION

As we saw, in considering the definition of a prostitute, the general idea appears to be that prostitution is exclusively a female profession. In reality, it is no such thing. There are male prostitutes in all large cities, and, although, owing to the different way in which they are regarded by society and by the law, they pursue their profession much more surreptitiously than do female prostitutes, those who are in search of the services of male prostitutes usually know where to look for them and are quick to recognise them. Actually male prostitution is as old as female prostitution ; indeed, the two branches of the profession have been coexistent in some form or other from the beginning of civilisation.

Homosexuality is common in almost every savage tribe. In many cases it is associated with the religious beliefs of the tribe, and sexual perversions form part of certain religious festivals and ceremonies.

In all religions, ancient and modern and the whole world over, in which celibacy is imposed upon the priesthood, homosexualism is rampant among its members, ranging all the way from mutual masturbation to the most degenerate of sexual perversions. Because of the opportunities religion affords for the comparatively safe practice of homosexualism, the clerical profession offers special inducements to congenital inverts and sexually depraved young men.

According to various observers, among the Pueblo Indians of New Mexico it was the custom in each village to keep a trained catamite or man-woman (*mujerado*), dressed in female clothes, and rendered impotent by long-continued masturbation and other practices, for the use of the bucks of the tribe on certain occasions. The *Mahoos* of Tahiti, according to Turnbull, writing some one hundred years ago, were men of effeminate appearance and dressed in woman's habiliments, who practised a profession he did not care to put into words. Klaatch and Roth affirmed that the *mika* operation* is performed for homosexual purposes, the men and boys who have been operated upon playing the part of the female to the other males and being said to " possess a vulva." Among the Dyaks, there are men who are dressed as women and used during the feasts for pederastic purposes. Some of these *basir*, as they are named, are, according to Harde-land, actually married to other men. Havelock Ellis, ** quoting Lasnet, mentions that the Sakalaves of Madagascar bring up certain boys, called *sekatra*, as girls, for the purpose of having sodomitical connections with men ; and refers to the boy

* The *mika* operation—sometimes termed Sturt's rite, artificial hypo-spadias, urethral subincision, *urethotomia externa*—is the slitting or puncturing of the urethra from or near the scrotum to the *meatus urinus*.

** Havelock Ellis, *Studies in the Psychology of Sex*, Vol. II., 3rd Edition, Davis, Philadelphia, 1926.

prostitutes of China, who, according to Matignon, are sold by their parents expressly for the purpose of prostitution, and after a special training, which includes dilatation of the anus, massage of the buttocks and removal of the pubic hair, " luxuriously dressed and perfumed," they are " ready to grace a rich man's feast." Westermarck* mentions professional male prostitutes in Bali, and states that homosexual love is prevalent among the Persians, Sikhs, Afghans and Tartars.

In the seventeenth century, according to Herbert, pederasty assumed such a degree of universality in Siam that in efforts to tempt the interest and attract the notice of the local male population, the young women walked about with their vulvas exposed.

Among the ancient Greeks pederasty was common, and male prostitution a most flourishing trade. We read in the works of Aristophanes : " And they say the boys do this very thing, not for their lovers, but for money's sake. Not the better sort, but the sodomites ; for the better sort do not ask for money." All the larger towns had special brothels where male prostitutes could be found, mostly young boys. These brothel-boys were for hire ; but in many cases the parents sold their boys at a tender age to become pathics for wealthy men. In ancient Rome male prostitutes were as numerous as female prostitutes. In fact, before and contemporaneously with the early days of the Christian era, pederasty was preferred to normal copulation. Almost every member of the aristocracy and all the leading lights in art and science openly practised

* E. Westermarck, *The Origin and Development of the Moral Ideas*.

it, seeing neither disgrace nor sin in such indulgence.

Male prostitution has always been a prominent feature in Indian native races, and, according to Burton, at the time of Sir Charles Napier's entry into Karachi, when he conquered Sind, several brothels, containing boy prostitutes and eunuchs, were found in the town.

In the Bible we find many references to the existence of male prostitution.* To some of these Biblical references I have already drawn brief attention (cf. chapter viii.) Most of the religions in rivalry with Hebrewism, particularly the Midianite and the Chaldean cults, were addicted to pederasty and bestiality ; and almost without exception, the temples which housed female prostitutes (*Kedēshōth*) also housed male prostitutes (*Kādēshim*). These male prostitutes, handsome, epilated young men, were dedicated to the service of the gods just as were the females. They were sacred men, and it was held that benefits were conferred upon anyone who had intercourse with them. According to Rosenbaum, the eunuch priests who were attached to the temples of Artemis and Cybele were sodomites.

Not unnaturally, some of these prostitutes, male and female, entered the land of the Hebrews and began to spread far and wide a knowledge of the more unnatural forms of sexual vice. That these practices were secretly indulged in is evident from the many references to the worshipping of heathen

---

* " And there were also sodomites in the land, and they did according to all the abominations of the nations which the Lord cast out before the children of Israel " (I Kings xiv. 24).

gods, and the persistence of strange and idolatrous cults in the land. Thus:

" But the high places were not taken away: the people still sacrificed and burnt incense in the high places " (II Kings xii. 3).

And thus:

" And they set them up images and groves in every high hill, and under every green tree: And there they burnt incense in all the high places, as did the heathen whom the Lord carried away before them ; and wrought wicked things to provoke the Lord to anger: For they served idols, whereof the Lord had said unto them, Ye shall not do this thing . . .

" And they left all the commandments of the Lord their God, and made them molten images, even two calves, and made a grove,* and worshipped all the host of heaven, and served Baal " (II Kings xvii. 10-12, 16).

A reading of the Old Testament reveals that the true worshippers of Jehovah viewed these pagan practices with repulsion and fierce resentment. They put into the mouths of their god the strongest condemnation of sodomy ; they threatened the vengeance of the Lord God upon anyone indulging in the worship of Baal or Moloch ; they meted out the direst punishments to men and women alike, whether of foreign origin or belonging to their own

---

* The " grove " (asherah), so often mentioned in the Scriptures, is the phallic emblem signifying the female sexual organ or yoni. Similarly, the frequent references to the " pillar " signify the male organ, or penis.

people, who were found practising these abominable rites. Thus we read :

" If a man also lie with mankind as he lieth with a woman, both of them have committed an abomination ; they shall surely be put to death ; their blood shall be upon them " (Leviticus xx. 13).

And again :

" And he brake down the houses of the sodomites,* that were by the house of the Lord, where the women wove hangings for the grove " (II Kings xxiii. 7).

And yet again :

" There shall be no whore of the daughters of Israel, nor a sodomite of the sons of Israel " (Deut. xxiv. 17).

In the New Testament, Saint Paul refers to the cult :

" And likewise also the men leaving the natural, use of the woman, burned in their lust one toward another ; men with men working that which is unseemly, and receiving in themselves that recompense of their error which was meet " (Romans i. 27).

It was the practice of sodomy which was given out as the reason for the wiping out of the Canaanites and the destruction of Sodom and Gomorrah ; and

---

* These men, *Kādēshim*, were attached to the temples and consecrated to the goddess, in a precisely similar manner to the consecrated women. They were male prostitutes for the service of the priests and worshippers.

there can be little doubt that the horror and fierce resentment induced by its practice, together with the fiendish nature of the punishment meted out to those caught practising it, were intimately associated with the fact that sodomy was indulged in by the followers of a rival and hated religious cult. Westermarck, who subscribes to this belief, points out that incest was evidently not looked upon as anything so grave as sodomy,* and the Roman Catholic Church considers unnatural intercourse to be a graver sin than incest. " The fact is," says Westermarck, " homosexual practices were intimately associated with the gravest of all sins, unbelief, idolatry or heresy."** This connotation between heresy and sodomy persisted for generations and coloured the reaction of Christianity and Mohammedanism to homosexuality—it colours the reaction of society and the State to homosexuality even to this day. The intimate connection between unnatural vice and heresy is clearly indicated by the fact that in the Middle Ages the same terminology* was employed in referring to both, and very often the punishment meted out to heretics and sodomites was identical.** In most cases this punishment was death, and, although in the eighteenth and nineteenth centuries, the extreme

* Immediately after the destruction of Sodom and Gomorrah, Lot committed incest with his own daughters.

** E. Westermarck, *The Origin and Development of the Moral Ideas*.

* Bugger, the English synonym for sodomite, derived from the French, *bougre*, according to Lea, originally referred to a member of an eleventh-century sect of Bulgarian heretics.

** The Zoroastrian religion, like the Christian and Hebraic cults, looked upon pederasty and other forms of unnatural intercourse as conclusive evidence of unbelief, and its practitioners as infidels.

rigor of the law was rarely inflicted, the death penalty was retained on the English statute book until as recently as 1861.

In all classes of society, and especially wherever men have been segregated, sodomy has been rampant through the ages. Michelangelo was a homosexual ; so was Frederick the Great ; so was Aretino ; so, too, Francis Bacon ; and so, unless the scanty available evidence lies, was Shakespeare. The *mignons* of Henri III. of France ; the " favourites " of James I. of England were alike notorious.

The causes of male prostitution come under three general headings : (1) The demand for the services of male prostitutes, owing to women being unavailable, usually where the sexes are segregated, as in army camps, barracks, prisons, *et al* ; (2) a preference for males, as in cases of true homosexuals who are antipathetic to the female sex ; and (3) the acquirement of sexual perversions by those seeking abnormal forms of sex stimulation, and in certain cases as a means of avoiding the contraction of venereal disease or as a contraceptive method.

In old and sexually impotent men, the male prostitute really finds the bulk of his clients. These clients may not be and probably are not true homosexuals at all. They are impotent so far as all response to normal sexual excitations are concerned. The causes are many. The subsidence of sexual potency may be the result of excessive coitus over a long period of years ; persistent masturbation ; or the use of mechanical or other aphrodisiacs. The role of the passive agent in pederasty is thus adopted as yet another means of producing sexual excitement in sufficient degree to induce erection.

The idea that male prostitutes themselves are all homosexuals is likewise a mistaken one. The majority are heterosexual men and youths who make a profession of the vice, and in most cases are prepared to take either an active or a passive part as required by their clients. The true homosexual is rarely a prostitute.

In Continental cities there are brothels exclusively devoted to male prostitution, which are known to and regularly visited by homosexual men. Other catamites frequent the hotels, making the acquaintance of homosexuals there. Others again secure employment as bath attendants—bathing establishments of all kinds and in all countries are rendezvous for homosexuals and hunting grounds for male prostitutes. In St. Petersburg, before the war, according to Tarnowsky, catamites charged the same fees as did the female prostitutes.

Despite the fact that sodomy is a criminal offence in Great Britain, there are large numbers of professional male prostitutes and secret clubs devoted exclusively to perverts, in London and other large cities, and in the University towns.* Actually it is extremely difficult to get any idea as to its prevalence. Convictions are rare and this gives rise to the false idea that homosexualism and male prostitutes are rare. But the number of blackmail cases which come into the courts, and the number

---

* Not all the catamites in University towns are prostitutes by any means. The notorious " fairies " of Cambridge and Oxford are not necessarily prostitutes.

of cases in which men are charged with offences against young boys, present sufficient evidence of the widespread nature of sexual perversion in this country.*

Prosecutions are made under the Criminal Law Amendment Act 1885, which provides that " any male person who commits or is a party to the commission of any act of gross indecency with another male person may be imprisoned for two years " ; or under the Vagrancy Act, 1898, wherein " any man who in any public place persistently solicits or importunes for immoral purposes, may, if dealt with summarily, be imprisoned for six months ; or if proceeded against on indictment may be imprisoned for two years, and for a subsequent offence may also be whipped."**

In countries where the practice of homosexualism is not a criminal offence, there are bars, night-clubs and dance halls where perverts meet openly. In Paris there are many such resorts.

There is another form of male prostitution to which reference must be made. In this case there is no criminality attached to it and no perverse practices associated with it. There are numerous young men who bear exactly the same relation towards wealthy women, as female prostitutes bear towards men. They provide nymphomaniacs, and

* There are many homosexuals and perverts who never practice true pederasty at all. In a large number of cases they are addicted to perverse practices which, although equally repulsive to normal-minded persons, unlike pederasty and bestiality, do not come under criminal law —thus coitus in os, perineal or intercrural coitus, and, most common of all, mutual masturbation.

** In practice the law concerns itself almost exclusively with the solicitation of men by men. Cases of men soliciting women are very rarely brought to the Courts, although the wording of the Act includes such solicitation.

other passionate or sex-starved women, with the sexual excitement they require. In Vienna these men are known as stallions (*hengste*). In some continental cities there are special brothels where women go to seek such partners. These male prostitutes also frequent smart dance halls, night clubs and restaurants which women patronise. The gigolo in many cases is nothing but a male prostitute.

The practice is nothing new. Wealthy Roman ladies regularly visited brothels containing male prostitutes. Each lady patron had her favourite, who was reserved for her exclusive use, his allegiance being secured by infibulation—a method then in common use to ensure sexual abstinence, and bearing a striking analogy to the female " girdle of chastity." In male infibulation the foreskin was drawn over the glans or end of the penis, two holes bored in the overhanging skin directly opposite each other, and through these holes, when healed, a metal ring or clasp was inserted which could be locked or sealed. While wearing the ring sexual intercourse was impossible.

Also there were libidinous females in Ancient Rome and Greece, and in certain Eastern countries, who had in their service circumcised* slaves and eunuchs for the express purpose of ministering to their sexual requirements. Among the Dyaks and

* The origin of circumcision is in some doubt. In many savage tribes it was, and is, undoubtedly adopted as a means of prolonging the sexual act ; and its justification among other races as a religious rite (Genesis xvii. 10) may have been merely a cloak to conceal its true purpose. The popular idea that male circumcision is restricted to the Hebrew race is a fallacy. It was practised by the Egyptians, Syrians, Phoenicians, and other pagan races and savage tribes in all parts of the world have been addicted to it.

other primitive races, the men who wear the "ampallang" (a pin or rod of metal, ivory, or bamboo, which is worn in the penis previously pierced for the purpose), or who fix feathers or bristles to the *corona glandis*, are said to be looked upon with especial favour by voluptuous females.

CHAPTER XVIII

THE LAW AND PROSTITUTION

PROSTITUTION is not a crime. In the modern
civilised State it is either recognised as a trade or
profession and licensed or regulated, as in the regulationist countries ; or it is treated as an evil to be
repressed whenever and wherever possible, as in the
abolitionist countries. Nor is soliciting a crime.
Nor is immorality.

In all civilised countries, owing to the fact that
the prostitute is treated as a social pariah or outcast,
she rarely gets justice. Many men and women,
who, in regard to most social problems, are reasonable and just in their reactions, the moment they
begin to consider the problems connected with
prostitution, become unjust, intolerant and vindictive. They would appear to be incapable of viewing
the situation without bias. The protection of young
men from consorting with prostitutes, and the
prevention of young women from becoming prostitutes, so engage their attention and warp their
judgment, that they applaud and encourage legislation which singles out for punishment and
ostracism one party to the contract while allowing
the other equally guilty party to go without any
form of punishment whatever and with an unblem-
ished reputation. It is because of this attitude that,

every year, in Great Britain, in the United States of America, and in other enlightened countries, hundreds of girls and women are punished by fine or imprisonment for acts which are not, in themselves criminal or legal offences—for soliciting, for importunity, for following the profession of prostitute.

In France, which may be taken as an example of those countries in which prostitution is licensed and regulated, the inscribed woman may carry on her profession without interference so long as she presents herself for medical examination at the specified times and places. The clandestine or unregistered prostitute, however, is in another and an entirely different street. She is, at all times, in danger of arrest, with subsequent inscription on the register. Her peril, in this respect, is intensified through the fact that, in addition to the persecution of the police, she is liable to be given away by the registered prostitute, who looks upon her as an unfair competitor.

In Great Britain, as we have seen, the only efforts in the way of regulation were short-lived ones which proved extremely unpopular. In comparatively recent years there have been various attempts to reintroduce some system of regulation, but they have all been defeated by the opposing bodies, mainly, as we have seen, on the ground that any system of licensing prostitutes is a licensing of vice.

According to English law, no action of any kind can be taken against a prostitute solely on the ground that she is a prostitute. For any steps to be taken against her she must have committed some other act which, either in itself or coupled with the fact of her being a prostitute, constitutes an offence. Actually, the prostitute is penalised to the extent that, although there is no law against her making her living as a professional prostitute, this very fact, in certain circumstances, may make her actions illegal. Thus an act which, in any other woman would constitute no infringement of the law, in the case of a prostitute becomes a nuisance and, as such, constitutes a punishable offence. In instance, a girl who works in a shop or factory can loiter about the streets and ogle men to her heart's content : the self-same actions on the part of a girl known to be a " common prostitute " is an offence in the eyes of the law. The Metropolitan Police Act, 1839, Section 54 (11), contains a clause which states that a common prostitute " loitering or being in thoroughfares* for the purpose of prostitution to the annoyance of passengers " may be arrested ; and a further clause (Section 54 (13)) reading : " Every person who shall use any threatening, abusive or insulting words or behaviour with intent to provoke a breach of the peace or whereby a breach of the peace may be occasioned," which has often been the ground for a charge against a prostitute caught in the act of solicitation. Similarly, Section 3 of the Vagrancy Act, 1824, has a clause which provides that " every common prostitute wandering in the public streets or public highways or in any place of public resort and behaving in a

---

* The act of loitering must be committed on public property. It is not an offence within the meaning of the Act if committed on private premises. It is for this reason that so many prostitutes make their overtures in arcades which are not public property.

riotous or indecent manner " may be considered to be a disorderly person. These are the clauses which have so often been invoked in charging prostitutes. There is no legislation against female soliciting *per se*.

Section 28 of the Town Police Clauses Act, 1847, contains a clause which reads : " Every common prostitute or night-walker loitering and importuning passengers for the purpose of prostitution in any street to the obstruction, annoyance or danger of the residents or passengers may be arrested by a constable without warrant, and on summary conviction be fined 40s. or imprisoned 14 days."*

In practice, however, to-day these clauses are rarely put into effect. There was a time, not so many years ago, when a police officer would arrest a prostitute for soliciting, and, on his bare evidence, would have little difficulty in securing a conviction. One or two recent sensational cases have changed this, and nowadays an officer must provide corroborative evidence. This is exceedingly difficult to secure. Few men will make a complaint against a streetwoman, however persistent she may have been in her soliciting. The result is that loitering for the purposes of prostitution, and open solicitation, are both common, as anyone can see for himself who cares to parade the short streets and the arcades in the Leicester Square and Piccadilly districts.

The more important Acts which deal with prosti-

---

* There is a measure, passed in 1825, which is still on the statute book, entitled An Act for the Preservation of Peace and Good Order in the Universities of England, in which there is a clause providing for the arrest of " common prostitutes " which are discovered in University precincts and are unable to give a satisfactory explanation for their presence.

tution are the various Criminal Law Amendment Acts. The original Act of 1885, for the passing of which the late W. T. Stead's sensational articles in the *Pall Mall Gazette* were responsible, raised the age of consent from thirteen to sixteen years.* This Act was strengthened in 1912, and again in 1922. It is so important in its bearing upon prostitution that it will be well to give here the main provisions of the Act as it now stands.

Criminal Law Amendment Act, 1885 (with amendments provided by the Acts of 1912 and 1922).

Part I.

Section 2. Any person who procures or attempts to procure : (1) Any girl or woman under 21 years of age, not being a common prostitute, or of known immoral character, to have unlawful carnal connection, either within or without the Queen's dominions, with any other person or persons ; or (2) Any woman or girl to become, either within or without the Queen's dominions, a common prostitute ; or (3) Any woman or girl to leave the United Kingdom, with intent that she may become an inmate of (or frequent—C.L.A. Act, 1912) a brothel elsewhere ; or (4) Any woman or girl to leave her usual place of abode in the United Kingdom (such place not being a brothel), with intent that she may, for the purposes of prostitution, become an inmate of (or frequent—C.L.A. Act, 1912) a brothel within or without the Queen's dominions, shall be guilty of a misdemeanour.

(A constable may take into custody without a warrant any person whom he shall have good cause to suspect of having committed, or of attempting to commit, any offence against Section Two of the Criminal Law Amendment Act, 1885, which relates to procuration and attempted procuration.—C.L.A. Act, 1912.)

* Until the passing of the Criminal Law Amendment Act of 1885, all sexual offences against girls came under the Offences Against the Person Act of 1875 (38 and 39 Vic., c. 94) whereby " to have carnal knowledge of a girl under twelve years was a felony punishable by penal servitude for life (maximum penalty,) and to have carnal knowledge of a girl over twelve and under thirteen, with or without her consent was a misdemeanour punishable by two years imprisonment (maximum penalty).

Section 3. Any person who : (1) By threats or intimidation procures or attempts to procure any woman or girl to have any unlawful carnal connection, either within or without the Queen's dominions ; or (2) By false pretences or false representations procures any woman or girl, not being a common prostitute or of known immoral character, to have any unlawful carnal connection, either within or without the Queen's dominions ; or (3) Applies, administers to, or causes to be taken by, any woman or girl, any drug, matter, or thing, with intent to stupefy or overpower so as thereby to enable any person to have unlawful carnal connection with such woman or girl ; shall be guilty of a misdemeanour.*

Provided that no person shall be convicted of an offence under Sections 2 and 3 upon the evidence of one witness only, unless such witness be corroborated in some material particular by evidence implicating the accused.

Section 4. Any person who unlawfully and carnally knows any girl under the age of 13 years shall be guilty of felony. Any person who attempts to have unlawful carnal knowledge of any girl under the age of 13 years shall be guilty of a misdemeanour.

Section 5. Any person who : (1) Unlawfully and carnally knows or attempts to have unlawful carnal knowledge of any girl being of or above the age of 13 years and under the age of 16 years, shall be guilty of a misdemeanour.

Provided also that no prosecution shall be commenced for an offence under Sub-section One of this Section more than (nine—C.L.A. Act, 1922) months after the commission of the offence.

(It shall be no defence to a charge or indictment for an indecent assault on a child or young person under the age of 16 to prove that he or she consented to the act of indecency.—C.L.A. Act, 1922.)

Section 6. Any person who, being the owner or occupier of any premises, or having or acting or assisting in the management or control thereof, induces or knowingly suffers any girl of such age as is in this section mentioned to resort to or be in or upon such premises for the purpose of being unlawfully and carnally known by any man, whether such carnal knowledge is intended to be with any particular man or generally :

---

* A misdemeanour necessitates application to a magistrate for a warrant a felony admits of arrest without a warrant.

(1) Shall, if such girl is under the age of 13 years, be guilty of felony ; (2) If such girl is of or above the age of 13 and under the age of 16 years, shall be guilty of a misdemeanour.

Section 7. Any person who with intent that any unmarried girl under the age of 18 years should be unlawfully and carnally known by any man, whether such carnal knowledge is intended to be with any particular man, or generally, takes or causes to be taken such girl out of the possession and against the will of her father or mother, or any other person having the lawful care or charge of her, shall be guilty of a misdemeanour.

Provided that it shall be a sufficient defence to any charge under this section if it shall be made to appear to the court or jury that the person so charged had reasonable cause to believe that the girl was of or above the age of 18 years.

Section 8. Any person who detains any woman or girl against her will : (1) In or upon premises with intent that she may be unlawfully and carnally known by any man, whether any particular man, or generally ; or (2) In any brothel ; shall be guilty of a misdemeanour.

Where a woman or girl is in or upon any premises for the purpose of having any unlawful carnal connection, or is in any brothel, a person shall be deemed to detain such woman or girl in or upon such premises or in such brothel, if, with intent to compel or induce her to remain in or upon such premises or in such brothel, such person withholds from such woman or girl any wearing apparel or other property belonging to her, or, where wearing apparel has been lent or otherwise supplied to such woman or girl by or by the direction of such person, such person threatens such woman or girl with legal proceedings if she takes away with her the wearing apparel so lent or supplied.

No legal proceedings, whether civil or criminal, shall be taken against any such woman or girl for taking away or being found in possession of any such wearing apparel as was necessary to enable her to leave such premises or brothel.

It will be noted that the alterations made by the Acts of 1912 and 1922 served to strengthen slightly the law in respect to procuration. Also the clause in the Act of 1885, whereby " Reasonable cause to believe that a girl was of or above the age of 16 " had been held to be a defence in cases under sections Five and Six, was, by the 1922 Act, restricted in its application to men of 23 years or under, and even then to first offenders only. Further, the Act of 1922 imposed much more severe penalties for keepers of brothels.

Turning to this aspect of prostitution, the keeping of brothels and the letting of premises for use as brothels, are prohibited in this country. Here the law is clear and definite. It is sufficient to be able to prove that various persons of both sexes are allowed to use the premises for the purpose of illicit sexual intercourse. There is no necessity to prove that the women are actually professional prostitutes ; there is no need to prove that the owner or tenant makes a profit out of those who frequent the premises.* But there must be more than one prostitute concerned. A woman may take any number of men into her house or room for the purpose of sexual intercourse without interference from the law.** But if two women conjointly occupy premises of any kind, and under any pretence, in which they carry on the profession of prostitution, these premises become a brothel. At the same time a police officer cannot raid premises suspected of being used for the purposes of a brothel

* In a case before Mr. Justice Grove, in 1882, the learned judge said : " What needs only to be proved is this, namely, that the premises are kept knowingly for the purpose of people having illicit sexual connections there."

** A house in which a number of prostitutes have *separate* rooms or apartments, where the owner of the premises does not live in them or have control over the inmates, is not a brothel within the meaning of the Act. A hotel, however, in which rooms were knowingly rented to prostitutes for the purposes of their profession would constitute a brothel.

merely through witnessing the disappearance within the doors of a few couples. The premises must be kept under observation for six consecutive nights. And, according to Bishop,* there are wily brothel-keepers in London who pursue their calling indefinitely and under the very eyes of the police, having several different houses, and never using any one of these on six consecutive nights.

There are, too, many establishments which, although they are virtually brothels existing solely for the purposes of prostitution, manage to evade the law by various expedients. There are " employment agencies," " service flats," " dancing academies," " massage parlours," " manicure and lady-barbering establishments," " turkish baths," " language-schools," " teashops," *et al*, where appointments are made and the girls sally forth when their services are required. There is no actual prostitution or immoral behaviour *on the premises*, and the police, even if they suspect the place, are helpless.

The Licensing Consolidation Act, 1910, contains a prohibitory clause against a licensee allowing his premises " to be a brothel " and from " knowingly permitting " known prostitutes to make it a " habitual resort." This does not mean that a prostitute must not be allowed to enter a public-house, but the provisions of the Act are interpreted as allowing her to remain in the premises long enough to consume one drink only. The Act can only apply, however, to such women as are known to be prostitutes by the licensee, and this fact in

* Cecil Bishop, *Women and Crime.*

itself largely nullifies the Act in the case of any public-house which is not too particular.*   On the other hand, it is this same clause in the Act which leads to over-scrupulous houses refusing entry to any woman unaccompanied by a male.

It will be noted that although there is no law in England against prostitution *per se*, there is a special and discriminatory manner of interpreting the public behaviour of prostitutes so as to render them liable to punishment or fines, virtually owing to the fact that they *are* prostitutes, and for no other reason, as similar actions on the part of other members of the public would not be proceeded against.   Such a possibility of interpreting a law leads inevitably to injustice and unfairness.   The question of importance in connection with the law as applying to prostitution is not so much how the law actually stands, as of what it overlooks or connives at in certain circumstances.   This is the position in every civilised country, and inevitably it means that the poor and the ignorant among the ranks of prostitutes have to bear their more successful sister's cross as well as their own.

The really stringent enactments are those affecting third parties making a profit out of prostitution, as in the case of the brothel-keepers already referred to, and those living on the immoral earnings of women or participating in the so-called " white slave traffic." The Vagrancy Act, 1898, and the Immoral Traffic (Scotland) Act, impose penalties of im-

---

* There are many bars in London and in provincial cities where prostitutes are nightly customers and may be seen drinking openly.

prisonment for males " knowingly living on the earnings of a prostitute," and the Children's (Employment Abroad) Act, 1913, makes the securing of a license necessary for anyone wishing to take girls under 16 years of age out of the country for the purposes of " singing, playing, performing or being exhibited for profit."

Other Acts containing clauses dealing with prostitution are the Burgh Police (Scotland) Act, 1892, in which Section 403 gives the police the right, with a warrant, to search " a house reasonably suspected to be used as a brothel "; the Children's Act, 1908, which prohibits the entry of children into brothels or from living with or being in the company of " a common prostitute";* the Aliens Act, 1905, which provides for the deportation of any alien who is convicted of soliciting or loitering for the purpose of prostitution to the annoyance of passengers ; and the Clubs (Temporary Provisions) Act, 1915, which was introduced as a war-time measure to prohibit the use of club premises from becoming the " habitual resort of prostitutes."

The profession of pimp, or living upon the earnings of a prostitute, is dealt with under the Vagrancy Act, 1898, which provides that " every male person who knowingly lives wholly or in part on the earnings of prostitution shall be deemed a rogue and vagabond within the meaning of the

* An exception is made in the case of the child of a prostitute, which may live with its mother up to the age of 14 years, provided she " exercises proper guardianship and due care to protect the child from contamination."

Vagrancy Act, 1824, and may be dealt with accordingly." The fact that a man lives with or is " habitually in the company of a prostitute and has no visible means of subsistence" is sufficient evidence that he knowingly lives " on the earnings of prostitution." Despite the law, however, pimps are everywhere. They are mostly married to the prostitutes who are working for them, and run some sort of business or agency as a blind. In all such cases the police are practically powerless. It is exceedingly difficult to make out any sort of case against a pimp who is married and is engaged in any kind of work or trade ; it is further almost impossible to charge a married woman as a prostitute.

Turning to the United States, we find that prostitution is dealt with by the Federal Law ; and, in addition, each State has its own supplementary law or laws. Prosecutions are generally made under the Vagrancy Acts, involving the taking of fingerprints, compulsory medical examination, and imprisonment in either a workhouse or a reformatory. As fornication itself is a criminal offence according to American law, in many States the mere fact of a man and woman who are unmarried having intercourse may lead to the woman being proceeded against and classed as a prostitute.

The outstanding feature of almost all legislation concerned directly or indirectly with prostitution is that the law is concerned with penalising, where there is any such intent, or regulating, the woman's part. Although prostitution is essentially a dual affair, the law rarely takes any cognisance whatever of the man's share in the act.* Nor does it, in Great Britain, take any cognisance of fornication so long as the woman does not make of it a profession. If she has other means of support, whether it results from employment or private means or from marriage, there is no risk, whatever promiscuity she indulges in or whatever soliciting she may do, of her being proceeded against under any of the provisions of the various Acts dealing *inter alia* with prostitution. Even if she is a professional common prostitute and is known as such, the law can take no action against her for selling the use of her body in fornication *per se* ; but it can take action against her as a street-walker, and, in certain circumstances, as a brothel-keeper or for engaging in solicitation.

---

* In America, the notorious Mann Act makes it a criminal offence to take a woman into another State for the purpose of fornication. The question of whether the woman goes voluntarily or is transported against her will does not affect the matter. The Act was originally introduced in order to prevent " white-slave traffic," but has been interpreted as including ordinary cases of fornication committed after travelling to another State.

CHAPTER XIX

THE CASE AGAINST REGULATION

THE fight between those in favour of the regulation and licensing of prostitution, as in France and many other countries, and those who are against all forms of regulation, as in Great Britain, has, for the past one hundred years been a bitter and a hotly contested one. And to-day there is in existence, in this country, a very strong belief among a considerable section of the public that the registration and medical inspection of prostitutes on the lines of the French system, would be to the advantage of the community.

The struggle is really one between morality and health. For while a number of advantages are claimed for registration, the one outstanding plea which is tirelessly brought forward in its support is that the compulsory medical examination of prostitutes which goes with registration keeps down the incidence of venereal disease.

Sanger, who was an enthusiastic advocate of sanitary inspection of prostitutes, contends that although prostitution cannot be abolished it can assuredly be diminished to a very considerable degree both in its extent and in its evil effects, by the adoption of a system of registration and medical inspection.

We have already seen how the terror induced through the spread of venereal disease turned the public against prostitution, and, after attempts at suppression had failed, caused the introduction of regulation and medical inspection. Every country almost, at one time or another, in a fit of panic at the onslaught of syphilis and gonorrhoea, has experimented with sanitary measures—as we have seen, even England has made more than one ill-fated attempt.

Now the trouble with medical inspection is that although it sounds admirable, from a superficial viewpoint, in theory ; it fails dismally in practice. And the reason for the failure of every scheme that has ever been put into operation, is not far to seek.

In the first place, owing to the existence of a double standard of morals, which has been referred to again and again in this work, the medical inspection only takes into account the infected woman. *It entirely overlooks the infected man.* The argument is that if the prostitutes are kept free from disease, the men will be free from disease, too. It is a fallacious argument. It is fallacious because a huge percentage of venereal infections from which men are suffering have not been acquired from professional prostitutes at all, but from amateur prostitutes, who, whether or not any system of registration were in force, would escape the net, and so be free from any form of medical inspection.

In the second place, in those countries where registration and inspection are in force, the medical examination is necessarily a superficial one, and, in many cases is little better than a farce. Abraham

Flexner, who, in the course of his investigations for the Bureau of Social Hygiene (U.S.A.), witnessed the medical examination of Parisian prostitutes, says : " The inspections consumed from 15 to 20 seconds each, for vaginal examinations,' so read my notes made on the spot, ' it takes less time to examine one woman than it takes another to mount the examining chair and offer herself for examination despite the fact that her clothing has been adjusted before entering the room."*

Anyone acquainted with venereal disease knows how easy it is for cases, and especially for cases of latent disease, to be overlooked, and particularly so where such a superficial form of examination is adopted. Moreover, it is not difficult for a prostitute to conceal a gonorrhoeal infection,** which is by far the commoner form of venereal disease.

There is another evil and another danger connected with superficial, and therefore rapid, medical inspection, which are often overlooked. It is possible that, with such a system, the *incidence of disease may be increased*. As long ago as 1864, Tardieu and Giersing pointed out that syphilitic infection could be, and often was, transmitted from one prostitute to another during these medical examinations, by means of inadequately sterilised speculums.

The superficiality of the examination is very nearly equalled by the superficiality of the treat-

---

* Abraham Flexner, *Prostitution in Europe*, New York, 1917, p. 217.

** A thorough cleansing of the vagina with a plain or medicated douche shortly before examination would, in most cases, be sufficient. It was owing to this practice of destroying evidence of infection being so widespread among French prostitutes that several doctors recommended that each woman be segregated and kept under observation before examination.

ment. It is rare for a victim of syphilis or gonorrhoea
to be detained in hospital until anything more than
the local lesions are cured. In Queensland, for
instance, which has a system of State registration of
prostitutes and regular compulsory medical inspection, any woman found to be infected is kept in a
detention hospital, usually for a period not exceeding eight weeks. While, admittedly, it would be
quite impossible to keep all infected women segregated until the diseases were properly cured, these
superficial methods are of very small and questionable value.

Even were the examination more thorough, and
the treatment prolonged until all fear of infection
were past, the value of the system is shorn of much
of its reputed efficacy by the fact that a prostitute's
freedom from venereal infection to-day is no proof
of her freedom from disease to-morrow. It is
manifestly impossible to have a daily system of
examination. Usually these examinations are fortnightly or weekly, and obviously a prostitute,
immediately after being given a clean bill of health
from the medical examiner, may contract gonorrhoea or syphilis from an infected man and, in the
interval before the next inspection, may easily
infect fifty to a hundred others. In 1925, before
the Commonwealth Royal Commission on Health,
the Queensland* Commissioner of Public Health,
in his evidence said : " There is no guarantee that
any woman examined at 9 o'clock this morning will

---

* Queensland now has the unenviable reputation of being the only part
of the British Empire where prostitution is regulated by the State.

be free (from venereal infection) at 9 o'clock
to-night."

Again there is the fact, so often overlooked or
ignored by those who advocate regulation and
inspection, that a very considerable number of the
older prostitutes are carriers of infection, though
they themselves are apparently immune, presenting
no signs of venereal taint. It is owing to this that
it is impossible for any medical man to be certain
that a man or a woman is absolutely free from
venereal infection. Even a negative smear obtained
in an examination for the presence of gonococci
(the germs of gonorrhoea) is not positive evidence
of freedom from infection. A second, or a third,
or a fourth test may reveal the presence of the
organisms. In syphilis, similarly, until two years
have elapsed, it is impossible to certify freedom
from infection ; and although all outward signs
may have long since vanished, the disease may be
latent, and so give to the prostitute an immunity
against reinfection, owing to the fact that anyone
actually suffering from syphilis cannot be reinfected.* Thus a prostitute with syphilitic taint
could have intercourse with a man suffering from
syphilis in a highly infective form and, while she
herself would present no signs of infection as a
result of such intercourse, she would probably
spread the disease among a large number of subsequent clients.

This apparent immunity to infection, which so
many of the older prostitutes enjoy, is partly

* This does not apply in the case of gonorrhoea or soft chancre.

responsible for the statement that the incidence of venereal disease is lower among the inmates of brothels than among clandestine prostitutes. Most prostitutes avoid registration as long as they can. Apart from those who are detected, usually through spies, and forced by the police into registration, it is only when trade is bad, or when the woman's good looks are endangered through age or exposure, that she enters a brothel. And by this time she is usually immune to fresh syphilitic infections. Similarly, once a brothel prostitute finds she is infected, she usually attempts, and often succeeds in her attempt, to escape examination and consequent detention in a hospital (which is virtually a prison) for treatment. She moves to another town, and, if possible, to another country. Before regulations and restrictions respecting admission were tightened up, England was a favourite sanctuary for French prostitutes afflicted with venereal disease.

In addition to the very considerable number of women who manage to elude registration, there are thousands whom the police are powerless to arrest. In most countries the woman, to be registered as a prostitute, must be twenty-one years of age, as it is hardly likely public opinion would tolerate a procedure which would unquestionably force a huge number of young girls into a shameful trade. The result is that girls under twenty-one, in their thousands, and outnumbering the professional " ladies," carry on with impunity the profession of amateur *fille de joie*.

Moreover, for reasons which have already been given, any system of registration is restricted in its

application to the poorest and most degraded of
prostitutes. It tends also, by its very nature, and
by the life of the brothels, to degrade still further
those who are enmeshed in its clutches. A feature
of brothel life is that the prostitute has no power of
selection ; she is compelled to have intercourse
with any man, however vile or repugnant he may
be, and with an almost unlimited number of men.
It is no uncommon event for a brothel prostitute to
satisfy a dozen or more men in a single night.

One of the great drawbacks and evils of the
sanitary system is that it gives to men a false sense
of security. It has been stated as a fact—a fact
that will bear repetition in this context—that nearly
every man, unless he is drunk, who contemplates
seeking illicit sexual adventure, is in dread fear of
being infected with venereal disease. It is for this
reason that he makes frantic efforts to satisfy his
sexual cravings with girls of respectability, and that
he will so often run risks of another nature in
seducing virgins. But in many cases it is a case of
a prostitute or nothing, and so he will, in any such
case, prefer a woman who can show a clean bill of
health to one who cannot. Because of this, so many
Englishmen and Americans indulge in orgies of
immorality when they are in countries where the
registration system prevails. Those who uphold,
or favour, medical inspection, stress so fanatically
and so persistently the virtue of the system in
preventing infection, that there is little wonder the
average man accepts without question the popular
notion that the prostitute who can show a medical
certificate of health offers a degree of safety com-

parable with his own wife or his fiancée. In this very fact lies one of the most pernicious points attached to the whole system.

All things considered, therefore, the medical examination of registered women has proved a failure. Up to the year 1899, when the Brussels International Medical Conference was held, the chorus of opinion was in favour of medical inspection of prostitutes as a means of preventing the spread of venereal disease. The object of the Conference was to discuss the problem of venereal disease, and its findings left the position a confused one, and began to sow doubt among those who had been foremost in advocating medical inspection. And since that day the volume of doubt has grown with snowball rapidity, and more and more countries which for generations have been persistent advocates of the system, are abandoning it.* Even France, the regulationist country supreme, where the system has been in operation for over a hundred years, is beginning to doubt its value, and in several cities brothels and registration have been abandoned.

Other methods of dealing with prostitutes afflicted with venereal disease have been attempted. One of the most noteworthy is the notorious Page Law of the United States, to which reference has been made in a previous chapter. This law, from the moment of its birth, was doomed to failure. It was doomed for the very same reasons that are responsible for the

* The only British Colonies where brothels are now tolerated and legal are Zanzibar, Nyasaland, British Honduras, and certain parts of the Indian Empire.

failure of the State registration and medical examination of prostitutes in vogue in France and other European countries, and in Queensland ; and caused failure to attend the attempts in England in the nineteenth century and during the war. All these measures were, and are, half-hearted and hypocritical attempts to deal with the evil of venereal disease. The statements, repeatedly made, that such regulations are put into operation in the interests of the prostitute herself, are hypocritical statements—they are, in every case, methods devised to protect the prostitute's clients from infection. The government, in putting them into operation, is merely subscribing to the hypocritical sexual credo that is ecumenic throughout the civilised world.

From a careful consideration of all available evidence, it would appear that the regulation of prostitution fails in its main objective, to wit, the prevention or reduction of venereal disease. It is more because of this than for any other reason that so many countries are gradually giving up the registration system ; though in nearly every instance prostitutes are subjected to interference that is not extended to those engaged in any other profession, whether or not it is recognised as a trade or legal calling.

All attempts at regulation bring evils in their train. They penalise the prostitute herself to an extent which is altogether unjustifiable. They result in forcing many amateurs to become out-and-out prostitutes. They cause respectable girls to be forced into prostitution. These were the evils responsible for the public outcry which led to the repeal of the Contagious Diseases Acts of 1864, 1866, and 1869, and the Act of 1918. They are the evils which, some ten years ago, led to the outcry against the Women's Court in New York City ;* they are the evils which are inseparable from the putting into force of the Acts which purport to deal with prostitution in this country.

Thus the registered prostitute, deprived of every legal right, compelled to submit to humiliating examinations at regular intervals, in some countries twice a week, in others weekly, in yet others fortnightly, becomes ever more degraded in spirit and body. The clandestine prostitute, while free from these ordeals, is ever in fear of arrest and registration. The poorer the woman, the greater her fear, and the greater her degradation. The rich prostitutes escape police supervision or interference by plying their trade under various fancy names and thus escaping detection ; or by buying off the police ; or through the influence exerted in their favour by patrons situated in high places.

But more than anything else, the regulation of prostitution, by permitting and encouraging the provision of brothels, supports and extends the traffic in women. In the Annual Report of the Association for Moral and Social Hygiene, an organization deserving the highest praise for the

* The public exposure, in 1930, of the graft and gross injustice connected with the Women's Court in New York City makes sorry reading. It shows how a corrupt police force, in combination with crooked Court officials, were able to carry out a systematically organized campaign for bleeding to the last cent those who transgressed the law ; and how, in addition, a perfectly innocent girl could be " framed," bled, and publicly branded as a prostitute.

long fight it has waged against the injustice to, and persecution of, unfortunate women in all parts of the world, and for the major share it has taken in the campaign against regulation, occurs the following significant passage :

" Because Regulation no longer exists in our country we sometimes forget the vile and brutal thing it is . . . Where the State permits or licenses houses for the recognised sale of girls' bodies to men it cannot forbid the proprietors of such houses to use such means as they can devise to procure attractive young women to become inmates of these houses. Thus there can be no effective laws against traffic in women in a country which licenses brothels."

Without regulation and State-approved brothels there would be little or no traffic in women. This does not, of course, mean there would be no prostitution in the sense of individual or free-lance prostitution.

There are grounds for thinking that Flexner is right in his contention that, in many countries, the system of regulation is enforced with the object of providing the police with additional means of spying upon and tracking down wanted persons. He says : " I have in my possession a copy of a letter written by a morals policeman to a street prostitute working for him as a pimp."* And again : " At Frankfort I was told of instances in which it was found that police officers lived in the very houses to which registered prostitutes were referred."** The same authority quotes Reuss as

* A. Flexner, *Prostitution in Europe*, p. 272.   ** *Ibid.*

stating : " The medical visit is only the excuse made for arbitrary police power." Many prostitutes are compelled to act as spies for the police. Similarly sex perverts in high places—of which there are many—are compelled to work as spies or informers under the threat of prosecution.

CHAPTER XX

THE EFFECTS OF PROSTITUTION ON HEALTH AND MORALS

THERE is a popular fiction which comes to the front whenever prostitution is a subject for discussion, to the effect that once a girl has taken to the streets for a living she continues on a steadily downward path until, afflicted with those diseases which are supposed to be peculiar to her profession, she either dies in the gutter while pursuing her career, or ends her days miserably in a hospital or a prison. And there are still people who honestly believe that those afflicted with " the disease" in its graver forms, are finally smothered to save them further misery and their associates from infection.

Coincident with these ideas is the contemporaneous one that a street-walker's life is an exceedingly short one ; that few prostitutes ever make old bones. Tait, in his book, *Magdalenism in Edinburgh*, referring to this very point, says : " In less than one year from the commencement of their wicked career these females bear evident marks of their approaching decay, and in the course of three years very few can be recognized by their old acquaintances, if they are so fortunate as to survive that period . . . not above one in eleven survives twenty-five years of age ; and taking together those who persist in vice, and those who, after having abandoned it, die of diseases which originated from the excesses they were addicted to during its continuance, perhaps not less than a fifth or sixth of all who have embraced this course of sin die annually." Even so competent an observer as Sanger fell into this error. He computed that : " *The average duration of life among these women does not exceed four years from the beginning of their career.* There are, as in all cases, exceptions to this rule, but it is a tolerably well-established fact that one-fourth of the total number of abandoned women in this city die every year."*

Further, Sanger was convinced that every prostitute undergoes a good deal of mental suffering, and that the thought of her shameful, wicked life, with the inevitable pauper's grave ahead, is bound to hasten her end. It is truly a harrowing picture that he draws of these women decked with their " tawdry finery," wearing on their faces forced smiles, racked by " torments, physical and mental," with " breaking hearts," carrying on their " loathsome trade."**

In the literature dealing with prostitution there are hundreds of similar observations, all emphasising the fact that the prostitute's life is one of eternal shame, sorrow, and anguish, punctuated by recurrent attacks of disease, and culminating in early death. I neither blame Sanger and his contemporaries, nor the host of well-meaning reformers and

* William W. Sanger, *The History of Prostitution*, p. 455.
** *Ibid.*, p. 486.

moralists who have followed in their wake, for giving to the world these fairy-tales. Many of these pioneer researchers were misled by statements volunteered by raddled old prostitutes who, for a meal or the price of a drink, gleefully acted the role of a brand plucked from the burning. Many others, with the reformative urge big in them, deliberately suppressed the truth, and painted the life and ultimate end of the prostitute's career in lurid colours and in the approved moralistic manner. But nevertheless, in respect of seventy-five per cent. of these stories, they belong to the realm of fiction.

Actually, the truth is altogether different. The practice of prostitution, as regards the huge majority of women, is sporadic. It is essentially a profession of youth, and the relatively small number of old joy-ladies that one encounters on the streets is not due to most prostitutes dying before they reach middle-age or dragging out a miserable senescence in hospital, workhouse or prison, but, on the contrary, it is due to the fact that, in the main, they have deserted the profession in favour of some other form of employment, or in order to marry, long before they so much as approach middle age. In countries where there is no registration, and in England particularly, prostitution is mainly a temporary profession entered into either in the ignorance and glibness of sheer youth or as a means of tiding over a bad time, especially in those trades which are seasonal. To a girl in financial difficulties it offers an easy means of earning money when all else fails. A big proportion of this huge army of temporary prostitutes manage to conceal from their relatives or friends their mode of earning their living. Particularly does this apply to girls from provincial towns and country districts, who, lured by the attraction of London, have left home and failed to secure the kind of employment they aimed at. Others who have entered the prostitute's profession through being carried away by the glamour of it—for to the slum girls of London and other cities it *has* a glamour—once they become disillusioned, leave the ranks at the first opportunity that offers. Many, as I have intimated, marry ; many others become " kept women."

All seaport towns carry a big number of temporary prostitutes. The wives of seamen, in great numbers, pursue the profession of prostitute during the periods when their husbands are away from home. In the same way, the wives of soldiers on service abroad, are often to be found doing a bit of street-walking.

There are a proportion who do continue to pursue the calling of prostitute for years on end, and even into middle age. But, as I say, they are relatively few. These few are of two classes. And singularly enough these two classes represent members of the most extreme sections of the profession—the lowest class of prostitute and the highest. The low class harlots, such as, in regulated countries, form a big proportion of the brothel harlots ; and in countries such as England and America, are the sailors' women who throng the ports, and the more common paraders of the Leicester Square and the Bowery districts ; usually continue to practice their profession as long as they can charm men of the com-

monest brand. In many cases they prefer prostitution to any kind of work they could hope to secure.
They end up as scrub-women, lavatory attendants,
and the like.

At the other end of the profession are the very
highest class prostitutes, gorgeously upholstered and
perfectly mannered, who frequent expensive restaurants and night-clubs. The very success of these
women induces them to continue to practice their
profession over long periods of time. It is a fact
that in any walk of life success leads to continuance ;
failure leads to the seeking of other avenues for the
display of one's talents. The greater the success of
the prostitute the longer does she continue to be a
prostitute. True, with the loss of youth, good looks,
and attractiveness, success inevitably begins to
wane ; but by this time the successful *fille de joie*
has either earned a competence, and is able to
retire or go into some business or other, or she has
secured a permanent position as the mistress or wife
of one of her clients.

But, it will be contended, seeing that all prostitutes (*vide* public opinion and popular sex books)
are diseased, it is certain that a big number must
end up in hospitals and meet with early deaths.
The reports concerning the incidence of venereal
disease among prostitutes have always been enormously exaggerated, and to-day more perhaps than
ever before are they exaggerated. This exaggera-
tion, in every country in the world, is due to many
and different causes. Much of it is due to propa-
ganda, and, queerly enough, all propagandists who
concern themselves with the problems of prostitu-

tion, from whatever precise angle they approach it, exaggerate this prevalence of venereal disease. The regulationists exaggerate its incidence among unregistered prostitutes to give weight to their plea for medical examination ; the abolitionists exaggerate its incidence among registered prostitutes to lend support to their campaign against regulation ; the State, the moralists, the Puritans, all exaggerate its prevalence among prostitutes of any and every type, registered and unregistered, in efforts to frighten men from association with harlots and to obtain sympathy with and support for their war on promiscuity and prostitution.

There are ample presumptive grounds for believing that the incidence of venereal disease among shop-girls, typists, chorus girls, factory employees, servants and others, including a not inconsiderable number of girls in more sheltered walks of life, to-day, owing to the great increase in promiscuity among women generally, is much greater than it is among professional prostitutes. There is, too, the fact, to which I have already referred, that a very big proportion of prostitutes acquire an apparent immunity to syphilis, and therefore are not in any way indisposed or afflicted through having repeated intercourse with male syphilitics. Then, in addition, the point should not be overlooked (although it almost universally is) that the venereal infections do not give rise to such serious symptoms in the female as in the male. It is, I think, largely through a consideration of the serious consequences of venereal infections in the male that has arisen the widespread notion that prostitutes, in view of their liability to become infected, and reinfected, must come to an early grave. There are hundreds of females, both prostitutes and respectably married women, who have been afflicted with gonorrhoea for years and have no knowledge of the infection, there are hundreds of others who would have no knowledge of their condition if they had not infected some man or other. And once the primary lesions have healed, the same thing applies in regard to syphilis. Deaths directly due to venereal disease are much rarer in women than in men—the number of females who fall victims to G.P.I. is a mere fraction of the number of males.

In any consideration of the effects of the practice of prostitution on the health of the woman practising it, one must bear in mind that the prostitute is spared many of the trials which beset the married woman ; notably, even in these days of contraception, the dangers to health and life incidental to parturition. For few prostitutes have children. It is because of this that Acton says : " If we compare a prostitute of 35 with her respectable sister we seldom find the constitutional ravages often thought to be necessary consequences of prostitution exceed those attributable to cares of a family and struggles of labour."* Admitting that modern conditions of life have to a big extent reduced the travail of the married woman, and that the smallness of the family (where there are any children at all) has brought her risks and work in this direction almost to vanishing point ; it must also be borne in

* William Acton, *Prostitution, Considered in its Moral, Social, and Sanitary Aspects*.

mind that the professional prostitute of to-day, in comparison with her forbear of Acton's time, lives the life of a queen.

In any consideration of the sociological side of prostitution, its value as a factor in the reduction of crime must not be overlooked or minimised. Lombroso and Havelock Ellis pointed out the significance of this fact years ago. " Prostitution largely takes the place of crime in women, thus explaining why women seem less criminal than men."* Obviously, woman, granted the possession of passable good looks, has always at her hand something which, if the worst comes to the worst, she can sell. Equally obviously, when occasion demands, she sells it. And, in God's name, who can blame her ?

---

* Lombroso, *Crime, Its Cause and Remedies*.

CHAPTER XXI

THE FUTURE OF PROSTITUTION

THE outstanding point resulting from any study of prostitution as it stands to-day is that professional prostitution is declining. There are fewer prostitutes walking the streets of London, New York, Paris, or any other large city, than at any time during the past twenty years. There are fewer prostitutes in brothels, and there are fewer registered prostitutes outside the brothels.

It is contended by some who have studied with diligence the huge decline in the number of prosecutions of prostitutes under the various Acts,* that the professional harlot is well on the way to disappearance. But these figures are very misleading. I have already drawn attention to the continually increasing reluctance on the part of the police to charge women with solicitation, and the coincidental increasing reluctance of the courts to punish women for this offence. But there is, in addition, a much more effective reason for the

* The remarkable decrease in the number of prostitutes charged under the various Acts which deal, *inter alia*, with prostitution, is shown in the following statistics :

	England and Wales.	Scotland.
1900-1904 (annual average)	10,598	2,900
1910-1914 ,, ,, ...	10,682	2,077
1930	1,161	347
1931	1,303	401

remarkable decrease in these charges. The modern prostitute is much more respectable than was her prototype of twenty or even of ten years ago. She has been quick to accommodate herself to the changed conditions of the age. She is quieter and better dressed, she speaks better, she is rarely seen drunk on the streets ; she is much more circumspect in her behaviour generally ; she solicits, true enough, but she employs tact. In short, there are few prosecutions for annoyance and indecent behaviour, because only on rare occasions is there the one or the other. Usually the women who are prosecuted are old offenders who are charged again and again. Coincidentally the girl of respectability is more meretricious in her dress, appearance, and behaviour. The two, respectable woman and prostitute, more and more tend to meet on common ground. The old type prostitute who pranced about, gaudily and drunkenly, in the Strand, Leicester Square, Piccadilly, and Regent Street, is a thing of the past.

All of which does not mean that the world has become more moral ; that single men are becoming chaste ; that married men are content with their wives. To the contrary, there has been a huge increase in promiscuity among men and an even greater increase among women. It is this increase in promiscuity among women, and the marked decline in moral scruples, that have injured so severely the profession of prostitution. We have considered all this in some detail in Chapter XIV, and the results are that more and more every year is man turning to so-called girls of respectability in order to satisfy his sexual appetite, and less and less is he having recourse to professional fornicators.

The decrease, therefore, in professional prostitution is coincident with the extension of promiscuity between so-called people of respectability. Unmistakably the general movement is towards the conditions prevailing in savage and semi-civilised states of society, where there was no specific body of women, either set aside by the government or self-immolated through general ostracism, for the use of men. More and more is there a tendency towards promiscuity—not promiscuity between males and inferior women, whether professional or amateur, but between men and women of the same or equivalent social standing. It is a movement the significance of which seems to have been either overlooked altogether or grossly misunderstood.

Virginity among women is becoming something to sneer at. It ranks as evidence of lack of sexual sophistication, of loss of initiative in erotic adventure ; of a deficiency in that magic something popularly referred to as sex-appeal. Birth control, if it has done nothing else, has made possible the competition of the amateur fornicator.

It is easy to see how any increase in the promiscuity of women generally must have deadly effects on professional prostitution. Apart from the preference of most men for girls outside the ranks of harlotry, to which reference has been made in an earlier chapter, the matter is largely one of economics. It is much cheaper for a man to engage in sexual adventure with respectable girls, especially to-day, than with ladies of joy.

Q

Coincidentally with this competition from single girls in search of what, in the jargon of the day, is termed " a good time," there has, in the past decade, been a phenomenal increase in adultery. It is axiomatic that from the beginning of time adultery has been prostitution's greatest competitor. The rise of one has always been coincident with the decline of the other. Adultery has many advantages for the man. It is, with some sensational exceptions, much less costly ; it is infinitely safer ; it has charms which are unknown to the consorter with prostitutes. And, in certain circumstances, and in certain circles, it may become fashionable. It has become fashionable in both England and America during the past few years.

All these factors are affecting the prostitute's profession simultaneously, and, in consequence, prostitution itself appears to be in a state of transition. It is still, in its more open, more brazened and more meretricious professional forms, something to be sneered at, to be rebuked and to be assailed with moral strictures and indignation : in its veiled, euphemized and obreptitious amateur forms it is something to be overlooked and often enough encouraged ; to be garlanded with the propugnation of respectability.

The temporary respectability of promiscuity is nothing new *per se*. We saw an excellent instance of this in the manner in which, during the world war, in the blessed name of gratitude, girls of respectability, and even of gentle birth, gave themselves to the soldiers without scruple, diffidence, or stint.

Together and cumulatively, these new sociological conditions are reducing the number of professional prostitutes and making it increasingly difficult for those who are engaged in the profession to earn a living. The popular assumption that all prostitutes earn big money is a fallacy. There are girls by the score who tramp the streets in the Leicester Square or Piccadilly areas night after night without securing a solitary client. If anyone doubts this, let him accost a few of these girls around midnight and find out how many are willing to accommodate him for the night at a charge of fifteen shillings or a pound, or in a " short-time house " for as little as ten shillings. In view of the heavy expenses which all prostitutes who frequent the more fashionable thoroughfares are called upon to meet, these figures tell their own tale.

Increased prosperity would, of course, bring in its train an increase in the number of prostitutes. It always does. A war would cause an increase in prostitution. Again, it always does. But these factors, if they come into being, will result only in sporadic increases in the incidence of professional prostitution. In the ordinary course of events it would appear that the downward course of professional prostitution will continue. There is no likelihood of the factors which are inducing this decrease falling off in their effects or diminishing in extent ; to the definite contrary, there is every likelihood that they will increase in scope and effect, and of the extension of other disruptive factors which as yet are in their infancy. In instance, promiscuity in women is likely to increase, not only as a result of the new freedom, but also through the disinclination of men to marry at an early age ; the different outlook on adultery, which verges upon being approved by society ; and the vanishing of the social ostracism which for so many centuries has been associated with pre-marital sexual intercourse. In addition, there is the extension of both male and female homosexuality and perverse sexual practices, which to a certain extent are displacing prostitution.

It is a consideration of all these several factors that has led to the notion that professional prostitution may disappear in civilised States. It is true, as I have attempted to prove, that where all are practising what is virtually prostitution there can be no such thing as prostitution. Thus any considerable extension of the existing flagrant promiscuity among women of respectability would inevitably reduce prostitution to relatively small dimensions. But even so, it would not cause prostitution to disappear completely. And the reasons for this call for no very diligent search.

The promiscuity of the modern girl is a selective promiscuity. It cannot be denied that men are finding more and more that they can get for nothing what in previous generations had to be paid for. But this does not apply to *all men*. In the tremendous main, any such gratuitous sexual favours are restricted to young men, and usually to young unmarried men.

It is a well-known fact that the clients of prostitutes, in the great majority, are married men. They are married men who, for a number of reasons, find it necessary or desirable to seek sexual solace at the hands of women other than their wives. I have already, in the first section of this work, referred to the fact that a woman's sexual anaesthesia is often directly responsible for driving her husband to seek some other outlet for his erotic passion. A very large number of wives are inconsiderate. The inconsiderateness and selfishness of man where his sexual appetite is concerned, are made much of in books and sex guides, but both are at least equalled and very often they are excelled, by the sexual inconsiderateness and selfishness of woman. Most married women of all but the very poorest classes take the attitude that coitus is something to be indulged in according to their own appetites and inclinations—they overlook or they ignore the fact that, owing to man's different physiological make-up, in actual fact the man is often the party who should decide this point. The result of all this is that, after the first flush of sexual passion has spent itself, the male partner often finds his advances repulsed at the time when he is most desirous of intercourse ; more, in any but the strongly potent man, he may find advances made to him when he is not in a position to satisfy them. All these sexual disharmonies are disturbing and dissatisfying ; their cumulative effect is the breeding of indifference. The man, somewhat naturally, turns to a woman upon whom he can depend to satisfy his appetite at the time of its existence. He turns to the prostitute. There are too, the monthly periods when any woman resents intercourse; then there are long stretches when the pregnant woman cannot, with safety, indulge in the sexual act ; there are

times of illness. Some men, true enough, religiously
practice abstention during any and all such times.
But this by no means applies to all. The majority
either cannot or will not be abstemious ; they
patronise prostitutes.

The desire for variety, not only variety in women
but variety in coitus itself, leads large numbers of
married men to hie them to the merchants of
venery. Nothing becomes so dull as sexual intercourse with the same woman in the same way.
The lure of sex is largely the lure of the unknown,
and the lure of variety. In another work,* I have
dealt in a practical manner and at some length with
this subject, and I have urged upon married men
and women the need to cultivate and to practice
the art of love. Few married couples do. They are
content to let love die the death. Both husband and
wife are jointly to blame for this. The woman makes
no attempt to master the art of love and its connotations, including the provision, within all reasonable
limits, of such varieties of sexual expression as the
husband may desire ; while the man shrinks from
putting his desires into words ; in fact, in many
cases, he would, such is his hypocritical attitude
towards sex, resent the mere discussion with his
wife of any such subject. Instead, he visits prostitutes, who are willing to provide every sexual
variation he cares to name, and many others of
which he probably knows nothing.

In addition, there are those men, married and
single, young and old, who are sexual perverts and
desire the gratification of their appetites by perverse

* George Ryley Scott, *The New Art of Love*, 1934.

practices. They are incapable of having coitus in any normal fashion, or of being sexually excited in the ordinary way. Fetichists, sadists, masochists, and pederasts—there are many such. Their wives, their mistresses, their girl friends, cannot satisfy their desires. For one thing, they have not the requisite knowledge, these girls of respectability and of orthodox morality. For another thing, they would reject with scorn and indignation any instructions or proposals connected with such practices. In all these cases, therefore, resort is made to prostitutes.

It is extremely unlikely that women of respectability will ever compete with the professional prostitute in this matter of satisfying the sexual requirements of male perverts, senescents, and satyrs. For this reason alone prostitution in some form will survive. For this reason alone it will remain a social problem so long as civilisation exists.

INDEX